Wakefield Press

SHATTERED LIVES

Miriam Miller began work as a conference interpreter at the European Commission in Belgium. She has since written books and papers for multinational organisations and speeches for corporate executives and political leaders in Asia and Australia. She lives in Perth, Western Australia.

T0363955

SHATTERED LIVES

the human face of the asbestos tragedy

MIRIAM MILLER

Wakefield
Press

Wakefield Press
1 The Parade West
Kent Town
South Australia 5067
www.wakefieldpress.com.au

First published 2008
Copyright © Miriam Miller, 2008

All rights reserved. This book is copyright. Apart from any fair dealing for
the purposes of private study, research, criticism or review, as permitted
under the Copyright Act, no part may be reproduced without written
permission. Enquiries should be addressed to the publisher.

Edited by Jane Arms
Designed by Liz Nicholson, designBITE
Typeset by Ryan Paine, Bovine Industries, Melbourne
Printed in Australia by Griffin Press, Adelaide

National Library of Australia
Cataloguing-in-publication entry

Author: Miller, Miriam.
Title: Shattered lives: the human face of the asbestos tragedy/
                   author, Miriam Miller.
Publisher: Kent Town, S. Aust.: Wakefield Press, 2008.
ISBN: 978 1 86254 788 9 (pbk.).
Subjects: Asbestosis – Australia.
                   Mesothelioma – Australia.
                   Lungs – Dust diseases – Australia.
                   Asbestos – Health aspects – Australia.
Dewey Number: 616.2440994.

Government
of South Australia

Arts SA

fox creek
wines

For Ron

AUTHOR'S NOTE

Most of the research for this book took place in 2005. Since then, some of the compensation cases referred to have moved on. Some names have been changed in Chapter 10 for the purpose of identity protection.

★ ★ ★

Invaluable contributions to this book came from people who have experienced the asbestos tragedy. Special thanks go to Frank Marciano, Bruce Horgan, Ian McLaren, Joanna Ball, Lorraine Green, Fay Noble, Steve Aiberti, Tom Simcock, Kevin Saint, May Tyson, Terry Buck, Buddy Durand, Allan Shaw, Merv Whitehouse, Tony and Connie Lopresti, and Dr Greg Deleuil.

Thanks also go to Robert Vojakovic at the Asbestos Diseases Society of Australia, and Rosalie Evans at the Maritime Union of Australia, for providing background information and co-ordinating interviews with members of their organisations.

Ron Miller's steadfast support has made it possible to write *Shattered Lives*. The advice of Eilin Mangan and Dr Lizzie Finn was of great benefit in developing the work, and Jane Arms helped to bring it to completion.

Contents

FOREWORD

by John Gordon

The scourge of asbestos disease is a modern plague in Australia. It has its dark side – the reckless and uncaring attitudes of the corporations like James Hardie and CSR that caused it, and then sought to avoid the consequences – and the pain and desolation it wreaks. But it also has another side – in the courage and dignity almost universally displayed by its sufferers, in the inspiration provided by the love and devotion of their families, in the heroism of those who care for them and fight for them in the medical and nursing professions and in the Asbestos Diseases Society, and in the determination of their lawyers to achieve justice for them. This book uncovers both sides of these horrific diseases in a sympathetic yet stirring account. Australia needs to understand asbestos diseases like mesothelioma, its victims – working people and their families – and its causes and effects a whole lot better. This timely book inspires such an understanding.

PART 1

HIDDEN SECRET

1

Asbestos is a killer, but governments and construction companies in post-war Australia could not get enough of it. Restrictions on the use of building materials during the war had caused a critical housing shortage, just as the population was expanding and the country was absorbing a massive influx of migrants from Europe. The needs of this burgeoning population were pressing, so federal and state governments set about urgently commissioning the construction of houses, hospitals, schools and other public buildings. Asbestos cement was cheap in the fifties and sixties, and the architects, engineers, and builders who designed and developed these projects used it extensively. In that frenetic era, when Australia wanted to forget the war and rush headlong into prosperity, asbestos was known as 'the magic mineral'.

In the late 1940s, medical experts began to warn government and industry that workers exposed to asbestos dust risked lung disease and death. Continued mining and manufacturing of asbestos, they predicted, would lead to a catastrophe on a scale that Australia had never seen. By then, more than a decade had passed since British medical literature first identified asbestos dust as carcinogenic; this was confirmed in 1955 in an epidemiological report published in the *British Journal of Industrial Medicine*. By the early 1960s, people in Australia were being diagnosed with cancers caused by inhaling asbestos dust.

The warnings about asbestos intensified as evidence of its dangers mounted, but staff in government departments who were responsible for the health and safety of working people did nothing to prevent the disaster. Their apathy allowed asbestos companies to conceal the facts about asbestos from their employees – and their clients – and to continue to use the mineral despite knowing that it could cause cancer.

Trade union officials also failed to act. They claimed to champion the rights of all Australian workers, but they displayed a singular lack of interest in the asbestos industry where most workers were immigrants and conditions were filthy. By the 1980s, when trade union representatives finally began to pay attention to the asbestos calamity that was unfolding in Australia, the damage had been done.

The suppression of vital information by government and industry and the inaction of trade unions continued for decades. Meanwhile, thousands of people went on working in places where they breathed in deadly asbestos dust. These workers assumed that the dust was harmless, because they trusted their employers to protect them from injury. By the time many discovered that their trust had been betrayed, they were doomed.

Concealing the truth – knowing that countless lives would be lost as a consequence – was a crime. It was committed by company directors driven by greed, inept bureaucrats, and indifferent trade union leaders.

It is April 2005 in Perth. Late one Friday afternoon, just as a holiday weekend is beginning, a young man appears at the office. He is skeletal, sickly pale, and stands alone in a meeting room where photographs of asbestos mines and factories hang on the walls. He has come to speak to a lawyer to find out how he can claim compensation for his illness, so that his wife and thirteen-month-old child will have enough money to live on when he is gone.

His solicitor arrives. An older man with a lot of experience, he is momentarily taken aback by the emaciation of his client. There is no time to lose. He heads for a small office adjoining the meeting room to set out the documents for his forthcoming meeting. A doctor uses this office on Tuesday and Thursday mornings when the tortured coughing of his patients can be heard by everyone in the crowded building.

The young man waits to be told what to do. He holds himself very still to control his anxiety and clasps his hands to stop them shaking. Radiant autumnal sunshine floods through the window behind him, but it gives him no joy, only reminding him that his life will be prematurely taken from him.

'Well,' says the lawyer, motioning for him to enter the office, 'we'll just pop in here, shall we?' He speaks in a polished professional voice and is well versed in the art of dealing with victims of tragedies. His client responds with a shy smile. He steps into the office, and the door closes behind him.

This man is the eighth person suffering from the fatal asbestos cancer known as 'mesothelioma' to enter the premises of the Asbestos Diseases Society of Australia in the last ten days. He is dying because, as a boy of five, he liked to be by his father's side when he was renovating his house using asbestos cement. Twenty years later, the boy, now a man, has discovered that the dust he inhaled from those asbestos panels is strangling him. His life will soon be over.

Today this man is seeking compensation, although a payout will be of no use to him, other than to give him

5

some peace of mind. Claiming compensation is the only action he can take, but no amount of money can give him back his life. For such loss there is no consolation.

Next week more desperate people will enter this office seeking help. Day after day, they will arrive in dazed disbelief at what has happened to them. These were once confident people with hopes and aspirations; now they face death. They come here on a quest to make the unbearable somehow bearable, only to find that they must grapple with administrative, legal and medical tasks. They are someone's father or mother, husband or wife, brother or sister, son or daughter, and they must work quickly to help the families they will leave behind. The weight of the wrong they have suffered overwhelms them, and the callousness of those who sacrificed them so easily confounds them. They know that asbestos has shattered their lives, but they do not understand how it has happened to them. They wonder if they are to blame for their misfortune, as they are buffeted around in a turmoil of fright and frustration and grief.

In their search for answers, they turn their attention to Australia, the country they love. They dwell on its youthful optimism, sunny promises, and the boundless opportunity it offers, and they linger on the limitless space, invigorating freedom, and natural grandeur they have taken for granted. In their lonely place, they examine the beliefs they have always held dear about Australia and begin to lose faith in them.

At last the time arrives – months or years later – when they can look beyond their own loss and start to see in full what asbestos has done to their country, the community they live in, and their colleagues and friends at work. Contemplating this scene, they sense another kind of sorrow and within this general sadness place their personal pain and consider anew the senseless waste that they have witnessed. This is when they shake their heads and say to themselves: How did a land so fortunate let such a tragedy happen?

The main reason for the building industry's infatuation with asbestos was its effectiveness as a flame retardant – a huge advantage in a dry land prone to drought and bushfires. Other advantages included its resistance to cold, sound, acids, corrosion and friction. Asbestos was found in layers embedded in hard rock, and its great value was its fibrous nature. It was as flexible and tensile as human hair, and the fibre proved particularly useful in the manufacture of fire-proofing materials and to reinforce cement products, making them lighter, stronger and more durable.

The name of the mineral, which comes from the Greek *asbestos*, meaning inextinguishable, points to the unique properties that have made asbestos so highly prized since early times, even when its dangers were also known. The Roman historian, Pliny the Younger, noted that slaves who wove asbestos fibre into fabrics often became ill and died, and later that masters compelled their slaves to breathe through transparent animal bladder skins while working with asbestos to prevent them becoming ill.

Asbestos has always been sought after, but the rock in which it is found is as solid and dense as granite, making it difficult to excavate. In Australian mines, men drilled out the layers of asbestos while other workers smashed the broken rock with hammers until they extracted the fibre. In a mill close to the mine, the fibre was checked for dryness and quality and then packed in hessian sacks; when the sacks weighed 100 pounds (45 kilograms), they were loaded on open trucks for transport. The trucks transported the fibre directly to manufacturing plants nearby, or to the nearest port for shipment to cities around the Australian coast and abroad. At each stage of mining, milling, transporting and manufacturing, the fibre released clouds of poisonous dust. And wherever there was asbestos dust, people were in danger of inhaling it.

Australia began to import asbestos in the early 1900s. At this time, white asbestos was being mined in Canada, blue asbestos in South Africa; and asbestos factories, particularly in the textile and cement industries, were emerging in Europe, Britain and the United States. The first asbestos cement sheets imported into Australia came from France. Later, much larger supplies were brought in from Britain. More than 90 per cent of the fibre used in Australia was white asbestos, but the use of blue asbestos was also widespread. Brown asbestos imported from South Africa was the third type of asbestos in commercial use, although not in significant quantities.

The dust released by all three types was deadly, but the killer fibres contained in the dust were invisible to the naked eye. Blue asbestos fibres were especially lethal. Shaped like minuscule spears – long, rigid and sharp – they pierced the spongelike tissue of the lungs, penetrating it like steel barbs.

In manufacturing plants, asbestos fibre was used in numerous products, including pipes, building boards and roofing slates made of cement, and insulation materials, paints and adhesives. Products continued to be manufactured from materials containing asbestos until the mid 1980s – more than twenty years after deaths from asbestos-caused diseases were first recorded in Australia.

For several decades after the Second World War, asbestos fibre found its way into buildings all over the country. Entire housing estates were put up with asbestos cement building boards and fencing materials, and inside the houses there was asbestos insulation. Ceilings were sprayed with asbestos plaster, and the floors of kitchens, bathrooms and laundries were covered in asbestos vinyl tiles. There was asbestos in carpeting materials, in the cement floors of verandahs, and in garden sheds that were often built of prefabricated cement sheets. Domestic appliances which generated heat, such as steam irons and ovens, contained asbestos insulation, and an asbestos heat control mat on the stove top was commonly used in kitchens. In the food industry, ovens and cauldrons were encased in asbestos insulation to prevent food burning when it was cooked at high temperatures in the preserving process.

Merchant and naval ships and industrial facilities were all asbestos-saturated environments. A thick layer of asbestos insulation was routinely wrapped around boilers, pipes and cables on ships, in power plants, petrochemical facilities and factories of all kinds; and paints containing asbestos fibre were often used to seal the insulation materials. On ships, the asbestos-based acoustical plaster applied to ceilings was so soft that pieces continually broke off, creating lethal dust in enclosed spaces.

Asbestos was the wonder product after the Second World War, and thousands of people came into contact with it at work and at home. They did not know that breathing asbestos dust could kill them, because this information was withheld.

Asbestos was used so pervasively and for such a long time in Australia that we will never be able to get rid of it altogether. Factories, power plants, offices and homes still contain deadly asbestos fibres, and the earth itself is contaminated in some remote areas where asbestos fibre was laid underground to prevent water and sewerage pipes cracking in the parched earth.

The Australian continent is hot and dry for most of the year. Deadly asbestos fibres travel most readily through hot dry air, remaining in the environment in the air we breathe. People who came into contact with asbestos fibre were often unaware of it at the time because it was disguised in products and unnamed. People could not have known, or guessed, for example, that asbestos was a common ingredient in talcum used as a dusting powder in condoms. They did not know, or imagine, that cutting an asbestos garden fence with an electric saw could create enough poisonous dust to harm their children playing nearby, or that drilling a hole into an asbestos cement wall could contaminate their entire house.

In the home renovation craze in Australia, home owners passionate about optimising the market value of their properties are everywhere unwittingly disturbing asbestos fibre as they go about upgrading them. They do not know that they are putting themselves at risk, yet people whose contact with asbestos was incidental are increasingly suffering from asbestos disease. They are the new generation of asbestos victims.

Asbestos fibres lodged in the lungs cannot be dislodged, and diseases caused by asbestos cannot be cured. Over the years – twenty, thirty, even forty or more – asbestos kills by stealth.

'Asbestosis' is the most common disease caused by asbestos. People who suffer from asbestosis experience increasing breathlessness, fatigue and chest pain, as the steel-like asbestos fibres cause inflammation, scarring and thickening in the delicate lung tissue, until the lung gradually loses its elasticity. The inelastic scar tissue shrinks over time, reducing the capacity of the lung to function, but the damage can go unnoticed for years as the lungs have excess capacity. The progress of asbestosis makes sufferers more prone to illnesses such as bronchitis and pneumonia, and the scarring of the lung tissue creates resistance to the normal flow of blood. This resistance strains the heart, forcing it to work harder to push blood through the lungs. People suffering from asbestosis can live with a diminishing lung capacity for a number of years, but most come to rely on extra oxygen, often in the form of a portable cylinder with an attached breathing tube. In the final stages of asbestosis, sufferers are frequently rendered immobile and must remain connected to a stable supply of oxygen day and night. As they approach death, a clubbing deformity of their fingers may develop.

Asbestosis can lead to lung cancer. Smokers and non-smokers alike can contract asbestos-induced lung cancer (and may or may not suffer from asbestosis), but there is a substantial body of medical evidence to prove that smoking tobacco increases the risk of contracting asbestosis or other asbestos lung diseases by as much as 60 per cent.

Asbestos fibres can also cause pleural plaques to form. The plaques are hard, wax-like crusts on the lung. They can appear as one or two larger crusts or a number of smaller ones, but regardless of how they show up, they cause loss of lung function and reduced elasticity. It is not uncommon for people with asbestosis or other asbestos lung diseases to have pleural plaques as well.

Asbestos fibres can penetrate the lung tissue until they reach the pleura, the lung's outer lining. Once the double-membrane lining has been invaded by asbestos fibres, the malignant and aggressive cancer known as 'mesothelioma' can attack it. Mesothelioma can take a very long time to show up but, when it does, x-rays reveal the tumour rapidly surrounding the lung and crushing it. The tumour is rock-hard and, as it expands inside the chest cavity, it generates litres of fluid and squeezes the lung to as little as a quarter of its size. The accumulation of fluid literally causes the sufferer to suffocate, and the tumour can grow so large that it compresses the heart and sometimes pro-trudes in a sizeable lump from the person's side or back. The progress of malignant pleural mesothelioma causes sharp shooting pains in the chest, breathlessness, dramatic weight loss, persistent coughing, vomiting, bloating due to the fluid build-up pushing down on the abdomen, and disabling fatigue. Mesothelioma can also attack the peritoneum, the membrane lining of the abdominal cavity. People suffering from peritoneal mesothelioma experience intense abdominal pain, constipation and severe weight loss. Secondary cancers caused by mesothelioma can affect the stomach, colon, and rectum, and also the lips, tongue, throat, larynx, salivary glands and mouth. Mesothelioma has proved invariably fatal and remarkably resistant to treatment and pain control. It is a disease without mercy, the one most dreaded by people who have worked with asbestos.

Fibres can also be swallowed as a result of consuming food or beverages contaminated by asbestos dust. Ingested fibres can be absorbed into the gastrointestinal tract and then enter the bloodstream; once this happens, they can travel to any part of the body. Autopsies of asbestos workers have revealed fibres in the brain, liver, pancreas, prostate, spleen, kidneys and thyroid gland.

About a third of people who contract diseases caused by asbestos dust inhalation in Australia cannot recall any specific exposure to asbestos, but it is certain that, at some point, asbestos fibres were present in the air they breathed. The danger was silent, odourless and invisible, and they had no means of avoiding it.

Asbestos disease kills people slowly, painfully and insidiously, and sufferers often feel ill for a long time before they are diagnosed. They sense that their health is failing but cannot explain why, and their inability to identify what is the matter makes their lives a torment. They worry. They withdraw into themselves, and those who care for them can only look on in dismay. In some instances, the uncertainty, anxiety and isolation lead to depression.

The risk of asbestos exposure is real – not just for the

people who have handled asbestos in their work, but for everyone. In today's generation of asbestos victims, women are showing up in greater numbers, as are people who were exposed to asbestos as children.

The asbestos industry has caused misery on a monumental scale, but it could not have done so without the collusion of governments. The construction boom that began after the war lasted more than thirty years, until the 1970s, and throughout that period government departments were responsible for establishing and enforcing safety standards for building materials. In the course of their work, the public servants entrusted with these responsibilities would have had access to technical advice and been well aware of the risks involved in exposing tradesmen and labourers to asbestos products. It would seem that they regarded asbestos as essential to Australia's development and thought that the risks associated with it were acceptable. Like other industries, the asbestos industry produced what the market required. Governments were among its key clients and did nothing to discourage the use of asbestos.

At the beginning of the twenty-first century, 2600 Australians are dying of asbestos disease each year. Epidemiologists predict that the toll will exceed 60,000 in the first quarter of this century alone and that the impact of asbestos disease will not peak until at least 2025. The worst is yet to come.

Asbestos disease has killed people all over the country, especially in communities where exposure to asbestos dust has been high, but the killing goes on. Decaying building materials continue to release lethal asbestos dust into the atmosphere, and people continue to inhale the invisible fibres in the air. Some will not be affected. Others will die early, especially people who inhaled the fibres when they were children. Asbestos disease does not spare those who are strong and fit; nor does it distinguish between gender or race. It often strikes when the exposure to asbestos has been long forgotten, and it can affect any adult who has come into contact with asbestos fibres.

We cannot be certain how many people have been killed as a result of rampant asbestos use in the post-war era. But we do know that thousands are dying, and will continue to die, because the truth about asbestos was covered up. Their premature deaths could have been prevented if the use of asbestos had been prohibited once the dangers were known.

The cost of the asbestos disaster to Australian society is enormous. As a general rule, people suffering from asbestos disease require continuing health care, including repeated admissions to hospital, treatment with sometimes many drugs, and the services of psychiatrists and psychologists in some instances – all of which must be provided by the health system.

Asbestos disease also puts pressure on the social welfare system. Families affected by asbestos illness often find themselves in drastically reduced financial circumstances and turn to the state for help. Sufferers of asbestosis, in particular, may be eligible to claim a disability benefit for some years, until such time as they are entitled to receive a federally funded retirement pension. Many will turn to compensation litigation.

The task of the judiciary in managing asbestos litigation is increasing. Lawyers endeavour to settle claims out of court, but the complex issues arising from the asbestos tragedy can only be tested in a court of law. As the asbestos toll rises, so will its impact on the resources of the judicial system.

Employers shoulder the cost of increased workers' compensation contributions to provide for statutory payments for people injured at work. The insurance industry, which gives employers protection against personal injury claims, believes that its funding of asbestos compensation is unfair. The industry sees itself as having to pay for the upkeep of the compensation system and has proved systematically combative in its efforts to contain payouts. Inevitably, insurance companies are charging policy holders in the private and public sectors increasingly high premiums to cover the asbestos-related payouts they anticipate.

Businesses large and small, governments and tax-paying citizens are all bearing the brunt of the escalating asbestos bill in Australia.

Australia has been hit hard by the scourge of asbestos, but it is by no means alone. Asbestos continues to be used in much of the world, and the epidemic of asbestos-related diseases is a global phenomenon which is on the rise. The menace of asbestos extends worldwide, into general communities, and into every walk of life.

Asbestos companies are vilified as merchants of death, but the calamity they have inflicted on the world cannot be attributed solely to unbridled corporate greed. The industry flourishes where it receives government support, tacit or explicit. It is enjoying rapid growth in the developing world, but even in First World countries such as Canada, governments enthusiastically promote asbestos mining and manufacturing industries to increase revenue and employment. Meanwhile, the cost of asbestos compensation is mounting, owing to the increasing number of claims, the determination of asbestos companies to defend actions taken against them and the self-interest of the legal profession in prolonging litigation.

For many victims the process of claiming compensation is fraught, as the onus is on them to prove that their employer's negligence caused their injuries. This is in keeping with a long tradition of blaming victims: the idea that people become sick at work because of genetic weaknesses or poor general health remains prevalent, and workers are still perceived to be responsible for their own welfare. Nevertheless, the sheer scale of the production and use of asbestos makes it inevitable that people will continue to be diagnosed with the deadly diseases caused by exposure to asbestos and will seek compensation in ever greater numbers. It is estimated that the asbestos compensation bill in the developed world will exceed US$300 billion over the next three decades, but in the Third World, where asbestos activity is spiralling upwards, the fight for compensation by victims is just beginning.

The largest asbestos producers are to be found in Russia, China and Canada. Increasingly, they are marketing their products in poorer countries, especially in Asia. The multi-national corporations dominating the asbestos industry calculate that workers will be compliant and that monitoring of occupational diseases will be lax in countries where poverty is rife. In developing Asian nations, asbestos is marketed aggressively, and its use is increasing virtually unchecked. On the beaches of Bangladesh and Pakistan, where old ships are sent to be broken up for metal, in Indian and Korean textile factories, in the asbestos cement industries of China, Vietnam, and Thailand, thousands of workers have no idea that their jobs can kill them. By targeting developing nations with their lethal products to make up for markets lost in the First World, asbestos companies have adopted the same strategy as the tobacco industry. By moving from country to country to profiteer from a toxic material, the industry is spreading fatal diseases further and further. Its killing grounds are growing around the globe.

The evil of asbestos is destroying lives all over the world. But where are the accounts of the human face of this tragedy? What happens to people who get a killer disease after coming into contact with asbestos dust? People stricken by asbestos diseases die too young, but the stories they leave behind live on. Such stories are all too common in Perth, the asbestos cancer capital of the world.

The city of Perth looks out to the greeny-blue Indian Ocean. Its sun-bleached buildings stretch north and south along the white sands of the oceanfront and eastwards along the banks of the Swan River. Further inland a fertile plain is protected by an escarpment of purplish hills. Beyond there is only the desert that extends across the continent to the shores of the Pacific Ocean.

Perth is an isolated city, the capital of a vast and inhospitable territory where the rust-red earth harbours immense mineral riches. The wealth extracted from the ground flows into the city, keeping it buoyant and prosperous, but this robust prosperity has come at a price.

Perth has one and a half million residents, and another half a million people are scattered around Western Australia, mostly in the south-west coastal towns. Of all Australian capital cities, Perth has the highest percentage of residents who were born in another country – about a third – and many of these migrants took any job they could find when they arrived. Blue asbestos was mined and milled at Wittenoom in the remote north-west of the state, and asbestos cement pipes and building boards were manufactured at factories in Perth for the Western Australian market, the largest in the country. The people who worked in these asbestos industries were mostly European immigrants.

Perth's migrant communities have been badly affected by asbestos disease, but the intense and widespread use of asbestos in the construction of infrastructure, public buildings and housing throughout much of the twentieth century has left the entire Western Australian population at risk. As a consequence, people are dying of asbestos disease every week in Perth, and the city is fast gaining notoriety for its incidence of mesothelioma, the highest known rate in the world.

It is a picture-perfect afternoon in autumn, the best time of year in Perth, when the sweltering temperatures and blustery winds of summer are over. The sun still shines all day long, but the restive ocean has become glassy calm and the night air balmy.

It is Friday, and in a few hours people will escape from the city for the Anzac holiday weekend. Some will make the short boat trip to Rottnest Island; others will drive down the coast to the vineyards of Margaret River, or east into the picturesque Swan Valley. Those who stay behind will go to the beach, picnic by the river, or entertain in their backyards. On Anzac Day, thousands will throng to the city centre to watch war veterans march past in honour of those who fought, and died, on foreign soil.

At the Asbestos Diseases Society, the telephones have stopped ringing. The office is located on a busy thorough-fare, Main Street in Osborne Park, a 15-minute drive north from the city centre. Industry and commerce thrive in Osborne Park, where the traffic roars and road accidents are frequent. In recent times, new immigrants from Africa and Asia, the Middle East and the Caribbean have joined the Italians, Croatians, Macedonians and Poles who have lived and worked here since the sixties. On one side of the humble premises occupied by the Asbestos Diseases Society is a branch of the Commonwealth Bank, where the queue to use the automatic teller machine forms early in the morning; on the other, a garish tattoo parlour where the entry door remains open all hours and trade is brisk. Up and down on either side of Main Street business is lucrative in the many cafes and restaurants.

Late on this pre-holiday afternoon, traffic is speeding towards the nearby freeway access, and a diffident young man enters the office. A single glance says that he is very ill, perhaps dying, but his emaciated appearance is nothing out of the ordinary here. People come to this place because they are afflicted by incurable diseases, and all of them have a story to tell about how asbestos destroyed their lives.

Some people became sick because they worked in an asbestos industry; others used asbestos products in their homes or hobbies, unaware of the danger to themselves and their families. Their stories tell us what kind of people they were, how they lived their lives, and how their exposure to asbestos changed everything. Some stories relate to James Hardie, the company that dominated the asbestos industry in Australia.

James Hardie had two asbestos cement factories in southeast Perth. The Rivervale plant built in 1920 turned out pipes to fill orders for the large-scale development going on in Western Australia, including new iron ore mines and towns to service them. In 1951, a larger plant opened nearby in Welshpool. Piping accounted for most of the initial Welshpool output, but with the ever-expanding mineral resource activities and the accompanying rise in affluence statewide, the plant was soon churning out asbestos cement building boards.

Frank Marciano started working at the Welshpool factory in 1961 and stayed there until he retired almost thirty years later. Now in his seventies, Frank does not look nearly strong enough for all the physical work he has done. Arthritis wracks his slight body, there is hesitation in his hands and factory noise has robbed him of most of his hearing. Frank's habitual facial expression is one of bewilderment, as if he is at a loss to comprehend how the job he enjoyed so much ruined his health.

The few steps from his front door into his living room are sufficient to cause Frank pain, and he is glad to sit down on the sofa. Once seated, he places his feet together and lays his small hands in his lap. Frank's hair is still dark, though not full, and he wears it neatly combed back. His dress is also neat – business shirt, knitted sweater, tailored trousers and lace-up leather shoes. Remarking on the brightness of the light coming in through the window, Frank asks his wife to lower the Venetian blinds. Franca has done this many times before and is happy to oblige. A gentle, homely woman, she knows exactly how much light to block out. Her actions are considered, unhurried and have the effect of reassuring her husband.

In the semi-darkness Frank's living room becomes a haven of calm, a shelter from the outside world, where it feels safe to delve into the past. In this place, Frank can relax his mind and let memories come back. Sitting opposite him in her easy chair is Franca. She leans forward, expectant and alert. Time devoted solely to reflection is rare, but today Frank can take all the time he needs. There is no rush.

Frank arrived in Australia in 1952 when he was twenty-one and found employment as a labourer in the construction industry. Work was plentiful for nine years, but then building activity slowed down in 1961, a temporary dip. At the time Frank was working on the construction of James Hardie's state office building at the Welshpool factory site. One day his foreman warned him that he might be laid off, because work was running out, and advised him to be on the lookout for another job. Frank's first thought was to find out if there was a vacancy at James Hardie. It was a big employer with a reputation for paying well, better than most companies in Perth.

Frank was on friendly terms with Hardie's works manager, so he asked him if there was any chance of a job. The works manager said no, because the company had just laid off sixty men. Later that day, however, he spoke to Frank again. 'Let me know if you're ever out of work,' he said, and gave him the name of the man to speak to in the personnel office. Frank took his brother Rocco with him to the personnel office and both got jobs, Frank at Welshpool and Rocco at Rivervale. Their workmates told them how lucky they were, and they believed them.

Frank's first job was as a gardener. The Welshpool factory stood on 45 acres of grounds with large lawns, flower beds and lots of trees. The gardener responsible for maintaining the grounds had gone on holiday to Italy and never returned, so Frank filled the vacancy. The gardens were attractive, and management liked to see them well maintained. 'The outside area was kept very clean,' Frank says, 'no doubt about that.'

Frank enjoyed his gardening job, but he wasn't happy with the pay, which was a third less than he'd been earning before. He had a family to support, so he kept asking for extra work. Soon he was doing the courier run to and from the Rivervale factory and driving Hardie's trucks when the company's drivers refused to work overtime. After a couple of years, Frank started working inside the factory doing various jobs. He went on to become sub-supervisor, then supervisor, in charge of maintenance and waste disposal. He performed so well that the boss, John Reid, always greeted him whenever he came over from Sydney. 'Frank,' he used to say, 'show me what you've been doing. If ever you've got a problem, just get in touch with me.'

Sawing the cement pipes created a massive amount of dust, Frank recalls. Huge fans sucked the asbestos dust out of the production area and fed it into collection rooms; each was about the size of a standard living room and had as many as fifty calico bags hanging from the ceiling. The dust was blown into the bags, and workers shook the bags so that the dust settled and the excess fell into bins underneath. Sometimes a bag burst open, sending dust everywhere. Workers emptied the bags on trucks and covered the dust with tarpaulins ready for transport. The trucks took the dust away and dumped it at one of several rubbish tips used by James Hardie.

One day, Frank was instructed to go into the blue asbestos processing area to fix a crack in the floor where asbestos fibre was falling through. The room was completely cleared so that he could do the job, but the foreman operating the high-pressure machine forgot that he was there. 'I was working away,' Frank says, 'when all this fibre was blasted into the room. If it'd been water, I'd have drowned.'

He is adamant that neither he nor anyone else at the Welshpool factory had any idea that asbestos was harmful. Not even the works manager knew that asbestos was dangerous. Nobody knew. 'If we'd known,' he says, 'they'd never have been able to get people to work there.'

One of Frank's jobs was to crawl inside a 24-inch stormwater pipe to scrape out the asbestos sludge blocking it. The waste had become hard, so he had to hack it out, a job which took him four months. Later, the company bought a high-pressure machine to clean the mud out of the pipes before it hardened. Inside the factory there was also a lot of waste that had to be cleaned away. Each of the production machines had a series of large tanks for recycling. Sludge settled on the bottom and sides of the tanks, and the asbestos froth that formed on top of the water dried and blew around. The tanks had to be drained every day, so that the slime could be removed and taken to rubbish tips.

'We didn't have proper breathing masks,' Frank says, 'just paper masks, and with all that dust, those little paper masks were no use at all.'

Trucks loaded with blue asbestos fibre arrived regularly from Perth's port at Fremantle and from the mine at Wittenoom. It was about 1500 kilometres from the mine on mostly unsurfaced roads, and the trucks took three or four days to reach the factory. After the mine closed at the end of 1966, James Hardie continued manufacturing with asbestos fibre from Wittenoom for another year or two. Once the company had used up all its supplies of blue asbestos, it started making the Hardiflex building boards that would prove very popular.

'Hardiflex didn't have so much fibre and it was white, not blue,' says Frank, 'so it wasn't nearly so dangerous. Of course, we didn't know that at the time. We had no idea that asbestos could kill us, and that blue fibre was the worst.'

In 1976, Frank was promoted to foreman. As house-keeping foreman, he had his own office and twenty men working for him. He was responsible for all the cleaning and maintenance work throughout the factory and its grounds – a role in which he spent most of his time getting rid of asbestos waste. He also ordered supplies such as cement, which arrived by truck five or six times a day, and paper pulp, which was transported in containers from the port of Fremantle. He was considered one of the lucky employees, because he worked regular hours – from 7.45 am to 4.15 pm – whereas most of the men had to work shifts.

He liked his job, because he had to think and use his initiative, and he knew that management thought highly of him. The company paid for his home telephone, so that workers could contact him if there was a problem in the factory. 'Talk to Frank,' managers would say, 'he'll sort it out.'

Frank's only frustration was that he couldn't rise higher in the James Hardie organisation. 'I ran the best team of the lot,' he says, 'but the company couldn't promote me because I didn't have enough education. Foreman was as high as I could go. Some of the teams had quite a turn-over, but my men stayed with me, and we all worked well together. We had no accidents or injuries, even though we did some of the most dangerous jobs on the site. With more education, I could have been a manager.'

One of the problems Frank faced as foreman was unblocking the pipes that pumped asbestos fibre between the three factory buildings. Fibre accumulated in the bends in the pipes and caused blockages. When this happened, Frank went up on the bridge walk and dismantled part of the pipe.

'I had no protection when I went up there,' he says, 'and if there was a strong wind, the dust blew all over Welshpool. I'd say to the plant engineer, "This shouldn't happen. What are you going to do to stop it?" But he'd just say, "What do you expect me to do?"'

Frank was the eldest of four children and grew up in Reggio di Calabria, on the southernmost tip of the Italian peninsula. He lived in the small town of Delianuova, about 30 kilometres inland from the Tyrrhenian coast, and worked on his family's land just out of town cultivating wheat, corn and vegetables. At the age of eighteen, he went to work and became a baker. He stayed at the bakery until he left for Australia three years later. The local government of Delianuova tried to conceal information about the assisted passage to Australia, Frank says, because it did not want people to leave. But he was able to emigrate because his father mortgaged some of his land to borrow the money for his fare. When Frank arrived in Perth, he felt he had to get a job straightaway so that he could repay his father.

Frank set sail from Messina, the Sicilian port just 10 kilometres across the sea from Reggio di Calabria.

'The *San Georgio* came down from Naples,' he says, 'and there were about fifteen hundred of us aboard. We sailed through the Suez Canal and the Gulf of Aden, then to Colombo, Jakarta and Fremantle. The last stretch was the longest. I was getting a bit worried, because everywhere we stopped on the way to Australia gave me a very bad impression. Everyone else felt the same way. We kept saying, "If Australia is like this, we're going straight back." But Australia was very different.'

Frank joined his uncle in Collie, a coal mining town about 150 kilometres south-east of Perth. His uncle, who worked in the building industry, had sponsored his application to enter Australia. Within a few weeks, Frank was also working in the industry. Three years later his brother Rocco joined him in Collie; and in 1960 they moved to Perth where Frank's youngest brother, Vincenzo, joined them. Frank's sister, Domenica, stayed behind in Delianuova to take care of her parents.

Frank married the girl who grew up next door. He proposed to Franca when he heard that she was emigrating to Australia, and they got married a couple of months after she arrived in 1958. Shortly after Frank started working for James Hardie, he bought a house in

Perth. He had a job with prospects, a family, a home of his own and considered himself a very fortunate man.

This is when Frank finds it difficult to continue – when he starts talking about what happened to Rocco.

'Rocco and I were always very close,' he says. 'Wherever I went, Rocco went too. When I got a job at the bakery, it wasn't long before he joined me, and he carried on working there after I left. When he came to Australia, he was really happy. In Collie he got a job in the building industry, laying pipes for the Water Board. When I moved to Perth, he followed me straightaway. He was my little brother, my best friend. There was a very special bond between us, no doubt about that. We helped each other do jobs around the house and garden, and Rocco was always coming over to my house, or I was going to his. Our families got along really well, and we often went on picnics together.'

At the James Hardie factory in Rivervale, Rocco's job was to sort out different types of asbestos – white or blue, short or long – and pack the fibre into sacks according to type. The fibre was first shaken and loosened in a machine – a process that created a tremendous amount of dust – and the men working next to the machine had a quota of sacks they had to fill by the end of each shift.

'Rocco must have breathed a lot of dust in that job,' Frank says. 'We were so close that I never expected anything to happen to him. He was as good as gold, as strong as a lion, a very strong man. It was strange because, at the beginning, the only thing he noticed was that his stomach was swelling. He was so fit and healthy – didn't smoke, didn't drink much – that he couldn't understand it. He went along to his family doctor who sent him away for tests. I can clearly remember going with him to get the results of the tests they did on the fluid. I'll never forget that day. "Peritoneal mesothelioma," the doctor said. I got such a shock. I couldn't believe it. When I got home that day, I had to tell my family. It was terrible. Everyone was devastated.

'It took only three months for Rocco to die. Watching him die broke my heart. It was a shocking disease, and Rocco suffered terribly. Towards the end, he had a tube inserted into his abdomen. There was a little pump attached to it for the morphine. Without the morphine, the pain was too much. Rocco loved his wife and his two children and three grandchildren. He'd been looking forward to retirement and watching his grandchildren grow, but he missed all that. The doctor told him that he was entitled to make a compensation claim. What good was compensation to him? He had no chance to enjoy anything.'

Rocco died in 1999. After his death, Frank became afraid that he might go the same way. He began to imagine that he had swelling and pain in the stomach, so he consulted a specialist physician. The specialist found nothing wrong, but Frank remained uneasy. Having seen his brother die of mesothelioma, he was well aware that this was a sneaky disease that could come on suddenly. He also had little faith in what doctors said, because, year after year, the doctor employed by James Hardie had told all the men at Welshpool that there was nothing wrong with them. Later, many of them died of asbestos disease. Frank remembers that the doctor was Irish, a tall beefy man who always had a pipe in his mouth but told workers not to smoke.

'For a long time,' Frank says, 'it didn't help going to see a GP, because most of them didn't know much about asbestos diseases. When Rocco was alive, we always went to Sir Charles Gairdner Hospital together for our regular check-ups. The first time I went on my own, I told the doctor that he'd died. "How did he die?" he asked me. "Meso," I said. "Oh, that's a nasty thing," he said, but I thought to myself, You should have known. You should have investigated it.'

Frank no longer has chest x-rays. 'I've had so many x-rays,' he says, 'that I don't want any more. Dr Musk at Charlie Gairdner told me that I've got plaques on my lungs. I hope I don't have a problem, but meso is a funny thing. It's like a mushroom – it just suddenly appears and *bang*, that's it. Since Rocco's death, the worries about asbestos are always with me.'

Frank worries about the plaques on his lungs, but he has no other sign – as yet – that he might get any other asbestos disease. He also frets about the likelihood of his wife and children contracting an asbestos disease, because they were all exposed to asbestos dust. He points out that Franca washed his dusty overalls by hand for more than ten years, until James Hardie started laundering workers' clothing on the premises, and that his three sons could have inhaled some of the dust on his overalls when he arrived home. His middle son, Giuseppe, is the one most at risk, he thinks, because he worked as a mechanic and fitter for several years at the Welshpool factory.

In 1989, Frank retired at the age of fifty-eight, because of poor health. He would have preferred to continue working, but he was troubled by arthritis, headaches and impaired hearing. When Frank left, he received all his superannuation and holiday entitlements from James Hardie, and he believes that the company treated him very well when he chose to retire. By the time he left, the workforce at the Welshpool factory had changed. When Frank first started working there, most of the workers were European immigrants – Italians, Dutch, Poles, Yugoslavs and Hungarians. When he left, most of the workers came from Burma and India.

Crawling in and out of pipes contributed to his arthritis, Frank believes, but he has no hope of being able to prove this after failing to claim compensation for his hearing loss. A couple of years after he retired, he succeeded in getting a small invalidity pension. He dipped into his savings as well and managed to get by until he turned sixty-five and became eligible to receive the seniors pension.

Frank remembers that white asbestos was used to manufacture pipes at the Welshpool factory until 1986. Many of the men he worked with have died, but he is convinced that it makes no difference whether they worked with asbestos for two days or twenty years. He points out that none of the men who worked for him has become sick, even though they had the dirtiest jobs in the factory. 'But a lot of people have passed away,' he says sadly, 'and a lot are fighting for compensation.'

Not all of the Hardie employees who have died of asbestos diseases in Perth worked at the factories in Welshpool and Rivervale. Frank remembers that the workers employed by James Hardie to install corrugated roofing on large buildings such as factories and ware-houses were covered in dust during installation. Hardie also employed men to install upright fencing; by the time the company told the men to punch holes through cement sheets instead of drilling them, it was too late for many of them.

Frank also recalls James Hardie's rapid growth. 'Hardie was the kind of company that just kept building factories,' he says. 'Wherever it was doing a lot of business, it built a factory. After it built factories overseas – in New Zealand, Malaysia and Indonesia – its business just kept getting bigger and bigger.'

He is grateful that he has been able to travel since he retired. He took Franca back to Delianuova for the first time in twenty-seven years, and they travelled in Europe and Scandinavia together. He is also thankful to be alive. 'I'm luckier than some,' he says. 'I'm still living, and so is Franca. We moved to Rivervale thirty years ago, and we're still in the same house. We used to do everything ourselves, but with my arthritis and Franca's diabetes, we need a bit of help in the garden and around the house.'

With an effort, Frank stands up. He leads the way into the kitchen – ordered and immaculate – and opens the back door. Just outside the door there is a street sign that says 'Marciano Avenue'. At the Welshpool site, Frank explains, one of the roads linking the factory buildings was named after him – as a gesture of appreciation for his services to the company. When he retired, he asked to take the sign with him. Standing on the patio with his wife at his side, Frank becomes animated. His eyes are drawn to the sign. 'It reminds me of the old days,' he says, 'before all of this happened.'

The afternoon is drawing to a close, but the sounds of a neighbour's house being demolished continue. Here in Rivervale, as elsewhere in Perth, land is at a premium. At an ever faster rate, old homes on large blocks are making way for functional brand-new residences built close together to maximise land use. The original houses in this working-class area went up during the post-war era, so it is likely that most of them contain asbestos. In the process of demolition that asbestos will be disturbed. Sometimes precautions will be taken, but not always. Inevitably, particles of poison will be released into the air.

Frank takes one last look at the street sign before stepping inside. 'I don't bear a grudge against Hardie,' he says, locking the kitchen door behind him. 'They were a fair employer and promoted good relations between employees. We had an excellent social club at Welshpool, and I was on the committee for seven years. We organised a Christmas party for all the staff and their families every year. It was always a big occasion, with presents under the tree for the children. We also had an annual dinner dance, and I can remember organising one at the Sheraton Hotel. That was a wonderful evening, a great success. I liked working for Hardie's. They treated me very well, I have to say. I just hope that I won't go the same way as Rocco. That's all I ask for. Every day I say a prayer. "Please God," I say, "don't let me get meso.'"

PART 2

EPIC BATTLE

3

James Hardie left Scotland in 1887 to sail to Australia. Aged thirty-five, he travelled alone and took with him a sheaf of references and introductions to get started in his new life. Hardie had to leave home because his father could not support all three sons. In the eighteen years that James Hardie worked for his father, he had proved adept at managing the finances of his leather tanning business. He was the eldest son, the young man with the necessary drive and commercial ability to succeed on his own, so he was the one who set off for Australia.

In Melbourne, when he arrived, horses were used for city transport, and there was a strong demand for leather. With the experience he had gained in his father's factory, Hardie had the perfect credentials to set himself up in the leather trade. Four years after arriving in Australia, Hardie was doing well enough to take on a partner.

Andrew Reid was another Scottish immigrant in Melbourne with a head for business, but what really set him apart from other young men was his ambition. Fifteen years younger than James Hardie, he had grown up on a farm near Linlithgow and knew the Hardie family well. He had been working as a shipping clerk in Glasgow when Hardie emigrated, and the two men had kept in touch. In his letters to Hardie, he pressed him about employment prospects. Hardie replied that he could introduce him to shipping companies, but did not offer a position in his own business. Reid set sail anyway. When his ship docked in Swansea for repairs, he noted in his diary that the people there had 'no energy for business'. Throughout his three-month voyage, Reid studied shorthand, bookkeeping and mathematics, and he learnt what he could about Australia from books and his fellow passengers. He was twenty-four when he arrived in Melbourne and persuaded Hardie to employ him.

The two Scotsmen established James Hardie & Co. in 1892, but it was Reid who drove the fledging enterprise. In 1903, the company gained entry into the building materials market when it started manufacturing roof slates from sheets of asbestos cement that were imported from France. In 1912, James Hardie retired a wealthy man, entrusting the business bearing his name to the stewardship of Andrew Reid. Reid coveted a grand vision for James Hardie & Co. and his steely determination to realise his dream allowed nothing to stand in his way. With no constraints on him, he unleashed his zeal for commerce and propelled the company he controlled on a meteoric rise.

Reid travelled to Britain to buy machinery and equipment for a new venture. On his return, he set up a factory near Parramatta in western Sydney and, by 1916, the plant was producing asbestos cement building boards. In 1920 James Hardie died, but his name has lived on in one of Australia's most prominent public companies. In the mid 1920s, James Hardie & Co. moved its headquarters from Melbourne to the more commercial city of Sydney, where it soon made its presence felt.

James Hardie's Sydney head office, Asbestos House, made an unequivocal statement about the organisation it accommodated. Its cold and cheerless façade looked down with disapproval at the teeming street below, its miserly windows letting in mere slivers of light so as to keep the outside world at bay. From the beginning, the Hardie organisation had an unassailable self-belief rooted in the righteous severity of Scottish Presbyterianism. As it expanded, the organisation took extreme care to select staff who would willingly and seamlessly fit into its culture. New employees tended to be young and pliable, and many of the recruits were relatives, friends and acquaintances of existing staff, or men who had served in the military. The result of Hardie's personnel policies was an all-pervading, inscrutable culture of secrecy and the single-minded pursuit of profit. Hardie's early entry into the asbestos cement industry formed the foundation of its unstoppable success. It enabled the company to secure dominance of the building materials market, a position it maintained virtually unchallenged for most of the twentieth century.

Hardie continued using asbestos until 1987 – just three years before asbestos manufacturing was banned in Australia. A decade later, asbestos imports into the country were also prohibited. In the 1990s, at the close of the asbestos era in Australia, the Hardie conglomerate turned its attention to the United States, where its new cellulose building products had been selling well and profits were soaring. By changing the focus of its operations, James Hardie could also evade its Australian asbestos compensation liabilities. And so the company managed the move out of Australia quietly to avoid attracting the attention of the media and corporate regulatory authorities.

In February 2001, asbestos cast a sinister shadow over Australia. The Hardie group became ensnared in its own machinations, bringing it face to face with enemies – the trade unions and asbestos victims' groups – it had long eluded. The battle that ensued aroused collective passion among Australians. All around the country – from the eastern seaboard to the west coast, and the tropical north to the drought-stricken south – people voiced their concerns about Hardie's attempt to slip away from Australia leaving thousands of asbestos victims without compensation for the loss of their health and livelihood. Marches were organised in Sydney, Melbourne and Perth to protest against what was perceived as the company's conniving and trickery.

James Hardie's success in its early years was primarily the result of winning the many government contracts in Australia and New Zealand for sewerage piping. Cement – mostly in the form of pipes and building boards – was by far the most important Hardie product, the one that underpinned the prosperity of the group. Hardie never let any competitor threaten its stranglehold on the cement building products industry and showed a voracious appetite for acquiring other businesses. Timing also played a role in the fortunes of James Hardie. By the end of the Second World War, the company was a large asbestos cement manufacturer in Australia and New Zealand, and the building boom that followed gave it opportunities for spectacular growth.

Obtaining secure supplies of asbestos fibre caused problems for James Hardie and, in 1947, the company acquired a share of a South African asbestos mine (owned by the British group, Cape Asbestos) to ensure that it would have adequate raw material to continue its success. In post-war Australia, Hardie was poised to capitalise on the surge in construction activity. No one could have predicted then that the building boom would last more than thirty years. But it did, and it was the making of James Hardie.

At the Hardie cement factories, the raw material was delivered in hessian sacks. Workers emptied the asbestos fibre out of the sacks by hand and used pitchforks to toss it into a mechanical blender. After blending, the fibre was blown through a duct system into an 'asbestos room'. Once the room was completely filled, the doors were opened, and workers forked the fibre into wheelbarrows and tipped it on scales to be weighed. The fibre was then ready to be dropped into a mixing machine with water, sand and cement to produce slurry, and this thin liquid cement was processed through machines to form board and piping. Once these were completely dry, they were trimmed and machine finished. The boards and pipes that left the factories contained up to 14 per cent asbestos.

In the 1950s, huge tracts of land were set aside for housing developments. Houses could not go up fast enough, and the building industry was operating at such a feverish pace that James Hardie struggled to keep up with the demand for its products. Yet more raw asbestos fibre was needed, so the company imported substantial supplies from Italy to meet the spiralling demand.

In the fifties, builders were keen to obtain Fibrolite, the new asbestos cement board manufactured by James Hardie. Residential developments made up of identical Fibrolite houses were going up in towns and cities all over Australia; even the screens at suburban drive-in movie theatres were made of Fibrolite.

At the time when Fibrolite was a household name in Australia, James Hardie was already looking at ways to reduce its dependence on asbestos. In 1964, the company achieved a breakthrough when it launched Hardiflex, a new building board containing vegetable cellulose. Hardiflex contained less asbestos than Fibrolite, proved even lighter and easier to use, and became another hugely successful Hardie product. By the 1970s, Hardie was phasing out asbestos at its manufacturing plants and replacing it with wood pulp cellulose (developed with the Cape Asbestos group). By then, however, thousands of people had handled Hardie asbestos products and many would die as a result.

James Hardie's ability to secure lucrative government contracts and its effectiveness in persuading successive federal governments to keep it sheltered from tariff barriers were the main factors driving its growth. Until the 1980s, Hardie never held less than 70 per cent of the Australian market for building materials and, in some years, its share exceeded 90 per cent.

In 1962, after it was awarded large contracts to supply railway friction materials, James Hardie formed a joint venture with the British asbestos conglomerate Turner & Newall to set up a separate friction materials division. This became another significant Hardie business, one that would cause asbestos-related health problems for hundreds of workers employed at rail works and in the automotive repair industry.

In 1964, Hardie established an asbestos cement plant in Malaysia and, in 1972, it pushed into the Indonesian market. In 1977 it took over Wunderlich, its largest domestic competitor. James Hardie's dominant market position allowed it to dictate the price of building materials, a feature that was reflected in the company's growing profits throughout the 1970s.

Hardie's push into overseas markets was accompanied by efforts to improve monitoring and control of dust at its Australian facilities. The group claimed to safeguard the health of workers by imposing dust controls but, as late as the 1970s, when it was widely known that exposure to asbestos dust could kill people, Hardie companies were still advising tradesmen to cut asbestos cement products with an electric saw. In doing so, they promoted the most dangerous method of handling these materials among people who used them in their daily work.

Hardie's position on the asbestos cancer issue was made clear in 1974 when a senior employee said, 'The industry is well aware of the hazards of asbestos, but if we considered no more than its fire retardant properties and its use in brake linings, asbestos has saved more lives than it has claimed.'

In 1978, the group chairman, Mr John Reid, grandson of Andrew Reid, revealed the enormous reach of the Hardie group when he said, 'Every time you walk into an office building, a home, a factory, every time you put your foot on a brake, ride on a train, see a bulldozer at work … every time you see or do any of these things, the chances are that a product from the James Hardie group has a part in it.'

Hardie's hold on the building products market was such that, when it began to phase out asbestos, it did not loosen its dominance in the market. By 1983, when the transition from asbestos to cellulose was well underway, the group was making clear its intention to get out of the asbestos market altogether. Its profitability rose markedly as it weaned itself off asbestos and introduced a new range of cellulose cement products. But just as this changeover was taking place, Hardie's asbestos past began to catch up with it.

Bruce Horgan is sitting in a spacious terracotta-tiled cafe on a mild winter's morning. The cafe serves traditional Italian fare and is popular with staff of the Asbestos Diseases Society just up the road. Outside, the trucks and vans rushing to service local businesses periodically shudder to a halt at the traffic lights.

Bruce is a busy man who, at the age of seventy-three, has no intention of slowing down. He is a man with a mission, which is to stay alive long enough to give his fourteen-year-old grandson a fighting chance in life.

In his youth Bruce worked at James Hardie's Welshpool plant for a brief spell in between jobs. He soon forgot about the factory work he did to tide him over, but years later he received a brutal reminder of it. His stint at handling asbestos, he discovered, had permanently damaged his lungs.

Bruce grew up in the rural town of Wagin, roughly 200 kilometres south-east of Perth, where his father worked as a motor mechanic and ran a garage. The 1930s were lean years, however, and the business did not do well. In 1939, Bruce's father took the family to Perth where he joined the air force and trained to become a flight engineer. Two years later, he left for Britain to fight in the war. Talking about his father, Bruce gives a small shrug of his shoulders. 'I think he was supposed to be the oldest Australian air force man flying,' he says. 'At any rate, he was away for four years. I had two older sisters, and my mother had to look after the three of us on her own. When my father came home in 1945, he said he didn't want to stay with us. After that, I never had much to do with him. I don't think he was really cut out to be a father. He was the kind of man who was always with his mates and, basically, he just didn't want to grow up.'

Bruce's mother took her children to Sydney to escape the shame of not having a husband. In Sydney, Bruce started working when he was seventeen as an attendant in a mental hospital. 'I lied about my age to get in,' he says, 'because the minimum age was eighteen. Not that it mattered, because all they really wanted was someone with two arms and two legs. There were no drugs in those days, and some of the things that went on in that place were horrific. I've never forgotten what I saw there.'

In 1951, Bruce joined the Australian army and was sent to the war in Korea with the third battalion of infantrymen.

As a frontline soldier, he was sent behind enemy lines. Following one foray, he was among the seven men not killed or injured out of thirty-one. On his return to Australia in July 1953, Bruce settled in Perth where he did some casual labouring work. Then he got a job with James Hardie.

Recalling his stint at the Welshpool factory, Bruce says, 'The company mixed asbestos fibre with cement to make its building products. My job was to empty the fibre out of the sacks it arrived in and shovel it into a machine fixed in the floor. The machine could break up to 140 pounds [65 kilograms] of fibre at a time, and I used a pitchfork to throw in the fibre as fast as I could. It was a dirty job, extremely dusty, and I only did it for three weeks.'

Bruce left the factory to start a carpentry apprenticeship – an opportunity provided by the federal government as part of its scheme to assist veterans of the Korean war. He never gave the job at James Hardie a second thought, he says, not until 1982 when he discovered that he had pleural plaques on his lungs. When he was given the diagnosis, he was told that the plaques could develop into something else, though not necessarily. He continued to lead a normal life but noticed that he had less energy than before. 'I knew that my health would never be the same,' he says, 'but I was too busy with work and family to waste time worrying about it.'

A few years after he learned of the pleural plaques, Bruce was contacted by Luisa Formato, a lawyer from the firm Slater & Gordon. Luisa informed him that he had a registered disease for which he could make a claim for compensation against James Hardie. She told him to see her as soon as possible, so that he could submit a claim before the expiry date. Bruce did as he was told and took along the group certificate for his period of employment with James Hardie. 'I'd kept it all those years,' he says, 'and it did make things easier – at least it was proof that I was actually there.'

Bruce lodged his claim in time, but did not expect much to come of it. Two years went by without any news. Then, one day, Luisa telephoned again. She expressed frustration, complaining that, after all this time, Hardie's compensation offer was so ridiculously low – $10,000 – that she had rejected it outright. Bruce was surprised, annoyed even, that Luisa had not spoken to him before rejecting the offer, but said that he would wait to hear from her. The next time Luisa called Bruce, she had another offer – $80,000. She explained that he had three options. He could accept the offer, refuse it, or bring in a Queen's Counsel.

'How much would a QC cost?' Bruce said.

'About a thousand dollars.'

'Is that all? Well, I don't mind losing a thousand dollars out of this offer.'

Bruce went ahead, his case went to mediation and the result was an offer of $170,000. He could hardly believe it. The payout was much more than he had expected, and he was very grateful for it. Thinking about the protracted process involved, Bruce is convinced that one of the reasons he received a reasonable offer in the end was that he never pushed the matter. He lived modestly and money was not of great importance to him, so he did not feel the need to contact Luisa or anyone else to find out how his claim was progressing.

Bruce has come across a lot of people who have suffered and died because of asbestos. 'Most of the people who got sick settled for whatever payout was offered to them,' he says. 'They needed the money and didn't want to risk rejecting the offer in case they ended up with nothing. I think it would be fair to say that it was easier for me to get compo because I'm Australian. A lot of people who've been affected by asbestos are foreigners who came to live here, and there's no doubt in my mind that they're at a disadvantage.'

In dealing with enquiries from around the country, in his capacity as a health inspector, Bruce finds that in communities where state legislation governing asbestos issues is inadequate, there is little he can do.

'Quite frankly,' he says, 'some communities are not being properly protected. In New South Wales, for example, if the man living next door washes his asbestos roof with a high-pressure hose and splashes asbestos all over your property, there's absolutely nothing you can do about it if he's a workman paid by a boss. Here in Western Australia the regulations cover everyone, whether they're home owners or employees. We have the best regulations of any state in the country. The state government body Worksafe covers regulations for workers, and every town has an environmental health officer.'

Bruce makes it clear that asbestos cement rarely poses a risk unless it is disturbed and that the softer asbestos materials, such as those used in insulation, are much more likely to do harm.

'That kind of material just disintegrates once it's disturbed,' he says, citing a case in Perth in 1984. 'We successfully prosecuted a popular night club which used asbestos plaster on the ceilings to reduce noise,' he says. 'When I inspected the premises, I touched the ceiling and the plaster just crumbled into my fingers. There isn't much of that kind of asbestos material left in Australia, except in some industrial buildings, but in Japan, for example, there's a lot of it. After the earthquake in Kobe in 1995, asbestos contained in the material wrapped around steel beams was released in massive amounts. Buildings were bulldozed, and the levels of asbestos in the air were extremely high.'

Bruce says that the asbestos cement many Australians are concerned about does not disintegrate easily, because it is hard, not soft. But he concedes that fibres are released into the air over a long period of time, as the cement deteriorates. The real danger, Bruce believes, arises when asbestos cement is disturbed. He identifies three main ways this is done: by cutting the cement with an electric saw, by sanding it and by drilling into it. Climate and location also play a role in releasing asbestos fibres into the air, he says. In buildings near the ocean, for instance, strong winds cause a more rapid deterioration of asbestos cement than elsewhere.

According to Bruce, one of the most common places where asbestos cement has been found in Australia is in public schools. Asbestos cement roofing was widely used in the construction of schools, he says, and, over time, acid rain caused the asbestos roofs to break down.

As far as asbestos in family houses goes, Bruce believes that the greatest danger is outside. When people paint an asbestos cement fence, for example, they tend to sand it down first, and the sanding of the cement releases asbestos fibres into the air. Inside houses, the danger from asbestos is mainly in wet areas such as laundries and bathrooms where moisture causes asbestos wallboards to deteriorate.

Bruce has looked at hundreds of state schools and government housing, including housing for police officers in Geraldton and holiday homes on Rottnest Island. He says the government of Western Australia used asbestos widely until as late as 1985.

In 1993, workers on Rottnest Island contacted Bruce, because they were concerned about the presence of asbestos. Bruce's inspections there since suggest that its environment may not be as pristine as previously thought. After his first inspection, Bruce warned the island authority that holidaymakers were being exposed to deadly asbestos and that deteriorating asbestos cement roofs needed to be replaced urgently. The authority made an undertaking to rid the island of asbestos, but made slow progress. Twelve years later, Bruce says, there is still a huge amount of asbestos to be removed from Rottnest Island.

Bruce has given presentations on the dangers of asbestos in the United States and Japan. He gives regular talks on the subject in Australian capital cities and lectures undergraduate and postgraduate environmental health students at the Curtin University of Technology in Perth. He has qualified as a carpenter, psychiatric nurse and environmental health inspector; and he is a Justice of the Peace and still undertakes judicial duties at Perth's Court of Petty Sessions. Whenever he gets the chance, he takes his grandson on holiday to Japan, Korea, Europe or the United States. He is determined to make the most of the time he has left, fending off his asbestos health problem with his extraordinary energy and will to live.

'I've seen what asbestos does to people for more than thirty years,' he says. 'Many times I've gone along with the president of the Asbestos Diseases Society, Robert Vojakovic, to act as a witness for signing of power of attorney when someone was dying in hospital. Every case is different, there's no doubt about that, but from all the cases I've come across, I'd say that there are two extremes. Some people are never affected, even though they were exposed to asbestos for many years, and others get sick because they had a very brief exposure. I can't say why it happens like this. No one can explain it, not even the doctors who work with asbestos all the time. There's still a lot we don't know about these diseases.'

4

James Hardie's reputation as a respected corporate citizen began to suffer long before the furore following its move overseas in 2001. The activities of Asbestos Mines, a Hardie subsidiary company, hurt a vulnerable community, one of the most disadvantaged in the country. When this became known in the mid 1980s, the decline of James Hardie's standing in the Australian community set in.

Asbestos Mines operated at Baryulgil, a remote area in northern New South Wales, where it employed local Aborigines to mine and mill white asbestos. For more than thirty years, the company did nothing about the asbestos dust at Baryulgil except undertake a cursory clean-up before official inspections. Consequently, dust rose up from the site continuously, and hung over it, a permanent haze of poison.

The Baryulgil Aborigines numbered about 200, and forty of them worked at the mine at any one time. The workers felt grateful to Asbestos Mines, because no other employment opportunities existed where they lived. Isolated as they were, the Baryulgil people did not realise that their jobs were killing them until asbestos disease began to devastate their community in the 1970s. Even then, they were slow to understand the effect that asbestos was having on them, because their mortality rate was already very high owing to lack of sanitation and poverty.

James Hardie decided to secure a domestic supply of asbestos when it experienced difficulty bringing in regular shipments from South Africa and Canada during the Second World War. In 1944, to obtain asbestos in Australia, Hardie formed a partnership with its competitor, Wunderlich, to establish Asbestos Mines. Wunderlich had been mining asbestos at Baryulgil since 1941 and continued to run the day-to-day operations until 1953, when Hardie bought its half share of Asbestos Mines. James Hardie then operated the company as a wholly owned subsidiary until it sold the site in 1976. Three years later, the mine closed.

Hardie was optimistic about Baryulgil to begin with, believing that it would produce enough asbestos to reduce its dependence on imports, but the mine did not live up to expectations. It performed poorly, producing meagre profits, and never became important to the Hardie business. Cement products were the real Hardie business, not asbestos.

Government mine inspectors had the habit of notifying management at Baryulgil of an impending visit. They did this to ensure that there would be no problem accessing the site and to maintain cordial relations with the managers. Having been warned that an inspection was imminent, managers ordered dust to be sprayed with water and the site cleaned. Throughout the operational life of the mine, inspectors made no criticism, and trade unions did nothing to improve working conditions.

The outcome of this neglect of Baryulgil workers – by their employer, government mine inspectors and trade unions – was a health crisis in the Aboriginal community that provided the mine's workforce. It took some time for the plight of the Baryulgil people to come under public scrutiny. When it did, controversy resulted.

In 1984, the government of New South Wales ordered an inquiry into conditions at the Baryulgil mine and the effects of asbestos exposure on the health of its workforce. At the inquiry, James Hardie maintained that it had done the Baryulgil community no harm and that its operations had been properly managed. It also claimed that the main reason it had kept the mine going was to provide jobs for its Aboriginal workers who would otherwise have been unemployed.

The media attention given to the inquiry further damaged James Hardie's reputation at a time when the number of its ex-employees being diagnosed with asbestos disease was rising. Public criticism of the corporation had been mounting before the inquiry, and Hardie had responded by establishing a workers' compensation scheme for former employees afflicted by asbestos disease. Unfortunately for the Aborigines who had worked for Asbestos Mines, their isolation and ignorance deterred them from coming forward with claims. They were of no interest to James Hardie, or to governments or trade unions. In effect, they were invisible.

Hardie stressed that its scheme was voluntary and that it had no legal obligation to compensate people it had previously employed. Those eligible for compensation under the scheme had to prove long-term employment with James Hardie and provide certification from the Dust Diseases Board that they were totally disabled by an asbestos disease. Many claimants had difficulty proving total disablement and therefore failed to qualify for compensation.

A couple of years after selling the Baryulgil mine, James Hardie was compelled to put warning labels on its asbestos products. Hardie had long resisted demands for labelling, but Australia was perceived to be lagging behind other countries in this, and regulations were brought into force. The labels had to include advice on how to handle and use products, but Hardie made it clear that there was no guarantee its recommendations would be followed.

Once labelling of asbestos products became mandatory, Hardie pressed ahead with plans to eliminate its use of asbestos and diversify into a much more broadly based building products business. Its new cellulose product range opened the way for its expansion into the United States where, in 1990, it established its first cement production plant in Los Angeles, California.

At the same time as Hardie was pushing into the North American market, it was becoming apparent that its asbestos liabilities in Australia would continue to increase dramatically. The group was still making small payouts from its voluntary fund (generally about $30,000 to individual ex-employees who satisfied the criteria for compensation) and also meeting the costs of judgments, settlements, and legal fees for common law claims as they arose. By 1996, however, it was obvious that, given the lengthy lead time of asbestos diseases, the group's liabilities would spiral.

James Hardie's success in the United States was such that, within a decade, it lost interest in Australia and decided that its future lay in America. It was concerned, however, that its continuing asbestos liabilities would make the company less attractive to overseas investors. To deal with this concern, Hardie drew a corporate veil over its liabilities, maintaining that its parent company could not be held accountable for the subsidiaries that had mined, manufactured, and distributed asbestos. Given the group's history of asbestos activity and dominance of the industry, the position it took to avoid its obligations proved untenable.

Asbestos liabilities stood in the way of Hardie's ambitious plans to push into the North American market. If the group wanted to achieve the tremendous growth it believed the United States offered, it had to divorce these liabilities from all its other activities. Making its mark in America was a design James Hardie held dear, so it set about solving the problem that threatened to jeopardise its plans.

Ian McLaren is 85 years old. He is descended from a family of Scottish slaters who came to Australia in 1856 from Comrie, a village in Perthshire. In his mid sixties, Ian retired from accountancy and sold the three tea rooms he owned in Perth, only to find that he could not slow down. In the early years of his retirement, he turned his attention to developing residential properties and did well. Looking back to that period of his life, he recalls how often he contracted builders to install asbestos roofs on blocks of flats. 'If I'd known then what I know now,' he says, 'I'd never have done any such thing.'

Ian still sees a lot of asbestos everywhere. At his bowling club, for example, he recently noticed that the rink was lined with what appeared to be asbestos, so he took a good look. It was definitely asbestos, he decided, because it had obviously been there for a long time, much longer than any modern material would have lasted.

His own exposure to asbestos was at home. In the fifties and sixties, Ian lived with his family in a prefabricated asbestos house overlooking North Beach, an outer northern suburb at the time. He believes that those years were the happiest of his life. He and his wife, Isla, let their four children play with their friends on the beach and in nearby bushland without supervision. Nowadays, Ian points out, the volume of road traffic in Perth makes it impossible for children to enjoy such freedom.

To give his children a playroom accessible from the verandah, Ian built an annex next to his house, on top of the asbestos shed. He used asbestos cement sheets to build the annex and put an asbestos roof on it. Inside the playroom, he put an asbestos dado around the walls and asbestos louvres in the windows.

Growing orchids is Ian's passion, and in his shed he made planter boxes for them, cutting and sanding asbestos cement with power tools. He also made seedling boxes out of asbestos cement. 'The shed was obviously a small enclosed space,' he says, 'and all the cutting and sanding made a lot of dust, of course, but I didn't think anything of it. When we shifted to a bigger house in City Beach in 1963, I threw out all the asbestos boxes and made new ones.'

The McLaren family moved house several times. Each time, Ian got rid of his planter and seedling boxes and started from scratch again. He made other things with asbestos cement as well, but believes that the letter box he made in 1965 caused his troubles. He remembers it well, because the cement was thicker than usual, about 10 centimetres, and he had to cut it into a number of small pieces. 'It was guesswork,' he says, 'and all the cutting created even more dust than usual. I really think that letter box was the start of what's happened to me.'

Ian thinks he became aware of the dangers of asbestos some time in the late 1980s. Having been healthy all his life, it did not occur to him that he might die as a result of all his handiwork. In the lead-up to his eighty-fifth birthday, he felt unwell and short of breath. He didn't think it could be anything serious, because his mother had suffered from shortness of breath for years before she died. He was looking forward to his birthday, however, and it bothered him that he wasn't feeling 100 per cent. He made an appointment to see his family doctor who sent him away for a chest x-ray and blood tests. Ian planned to do both that day, but did not manage to get a blood sample taken.

'That afternoon at twenty-past two,' he says, 'they took an x-ray of my chest. When the nurse came up to me afterwards, I sensed that something was wrong. She held the envelope containing my x-ray under her arm, as if she didn't want to let go of it. Instead of sending me away, she told me to go straight back to my GP. "I've made an appointment for you," she said. "He's waiting for you at the surgery." So, off we went. My GP said I had fluid on my lungs, and by five-thirty that afternoon I was in the Mount Hospital having a whole raft of tests done.'

Isla vividly recalls hearing the diagnosis. 'When I heard it was mesothelioma,' she says, 'it was such a shock I didn't take it in. I was speechless, and so was Ian. Even our GP said he was very shocked when he found out about it. It hadn't even entered my head that Ian would get an asbestos disease, because he was always such a strong active man. Even at his age, he didn't need to take any medication. Then, out of the blue, we heard he had this terrible disease. I'd spent my whole life thinking that I wouldn't have to worry about getting old, because Ian would outlive me. He was miles healthier than most people and never thought about his health, because nothing was ever wrong with him.'

Isla is right. Years of wholesome living have stood Ian in good stead, it seems, helping him to cope better with the ravages of mesothelioma than he might otherwise have done. His naturally thin physique disguises the onset of gauntness, his eyes retain the piercing blue of his Celtic forefathers, and the rosy tinge on his cheeks is yet to fade.

Isla's youthful appearance is also deceptive. The shock of what has happened to her husband shows neither in her face nor in her demeanour. She is a calm woman with abundant silver-grey hair and smooth skin. Taking care of her family has been Isla's career, and her gratification is the professional and personal success of her children. She knows that her children will lend her support once Ian is gone and takes comfort from this as she confronts the prospect of widowhood.

Soon after his diagnosis in June 2005, Ian started undergoing chemotherapy treatment in the hope that he might live longer, but he is frustrated by the unwillingness of doctors to discuss his progress.

'They're loath to tell me anything,' he says. 'I suppose they can't afford to say, "This might prolong your life," because they're frightened of insurance claims. Finding out what they're trying to achieve is like drawing teeth.'

The cost of his chemotherapy is mostly covered by Medicare, Ian says, despite the eighteen-week treatment being provided at a private hospital. One week of rest follows each two-week period of treatment but, if Ian doesn't respond well to the treatment, the following session is postponed. At each session, he lies on a recliner chair for three and a half hours as drugs are injected into his arm. He doesn't find the treatments uncomfortable, but the drugs have exacerbated his shortness of breath – an effect he hadn't expected – and made him feel tired and out of sorts. He thinks that the chemotherapy is largely experimental and has never heard any doctor mention a successful outcome. 'I'm no longer the bouncy person I used to be,' he says ruefully, 'but at least I can go bowling or play golf on the odd occasion.'

Isla mentions with some pride that she and Ian have been happily married for fifty-seven years.

'Our ambition now,' she says, 'is to live each day as best we can. We don't sit at home brooding about what we could have done differently or what might have been. We're both desperately sorry that this has happened, but we're dealing with Ian's condition in the same way we've tackled other difficulties in the past.'

Isla also finds the communication with doctors difficult. They do try, she says, but they can't actually say very much, because they don't know what the outcome of the chemotherapy will be. In the course of frequent hospital visits, Isla has met seriously ill people and has reached the conclusion that cancer among the elderly is prevalent. She has seen cancer sufferers maintain a cheerful manner when they have little hope of recovery and admired their resilience. What puzzles Isla is the apparent dearth of medical research into asbestos diseases. Some of the world's leading experts in this field are to be found in Perth, she says, so it's disappointing that more is not being done.

'There's an enormous amount of information available about cancers on the Internet,' Isla says, 'especially out of the United States. I try to keep informed about what to expect in Ian's case, what treatments are available, and what chance they have of success. Every week we get screeds of information through the mail from an Australian company about natural products which are supposed to cure everything. I look through all of it carefully, but there's never any mention of asbestos. When I was in our local pharmacy recently, I asked the chemist if natural products have any benefit over medicines. "No way!" he said. So, we're just continuing with the treatment and eating carrots, carrots, carrots, because Ian's been advised to take lots of Vitamin A.'

Ian had expected to live much longer. He concedes that this may seem strange to some people but, given his family history of longevity, he thinks it was a reasonable expectation. His mother was nearly a hundred and two when she died, and other members of his family on both sides have also lived to be a hundred plus. What worries Ian most is that his children's exposure to asbestos might affect them. He remembers how his children liked to help him when he was working in his shed, and he believes that they would have inhaled some of the asbestos dust present in the air. He knows that his children's concern has increased since he was diagnosed with mesothelioma, but takes heart that they are not dwelling on his condition and are getting on with their lives. One of his sons is away at the moment, sailing from Britain to Brazil in a round-the-world yachting event. Ian is pleased that he decided to go and is sure that he will see him return.

He is proceeding with a claim for damages against James Hardie.

'One of the specialists I saw suggested that I get in touch with the Asbestos Diseases Society,' he says, 'so I got on to that straightaway. The first person I spoke to was Rose Marie Vojakovic, the wife of the president, Robert Vojakovic. I found her very helpful indeed.

'Robert is quite often in the newspapers or on television commenting on asbestos issues. Without his efforts I really think asbestos victims in Australia would have had a much more difficult time getting compensation for what's happened to them. I think that Robert and his team are really taking the weight of decisions off victims' shoulders. Rose Marie pointed me in the right direction without making me fish for information and put me in touch with the law firm Slater & Gordon to see about compensation.

'At Slater & Gordon the lawyer is a young man called Tim Hammond who doesn't waste any time. This surprised me, frankly, because it's been my experience that solicitors always waste time if they can. I was diagnosed quite early, which makes things easier. I suppose there's always a sense of urgency in asbestos cases because so many people have died before their claims could be settled, but my own case has been very quick-moving. I've been very impressed by Slater & Gordon – they've been straight-forward, thorough, professional, and on the ball.'

Ian cannot categorically claim that a James Hardie product caused him to contract mesothelioma. Hardie was the only manufacturer of the asbestos products he habitually used, however, so it can be inferred that one of the company's products caused his cancer. He believes that his case is straightforward – he did not work with asbestos, therefore the only way he could have contracted mesothelioma was by using an asbestos product. He is also confident about the outcome and does not expect the opposing lawyers to put up much of a fight about whether the Hardie products were the only ones available or not. If the claim is successful, all his medical expenses covered by Medicare and his private health insurer up to the date of settlement will be deducted from his payout.

Ian regards any compensation he may receive as recognition of the harm done to him, although it would also give his wife greater financial security. Compensation was not something he had thought about until very recently, he says, when he calculated how much it would cost Isla to live on her own and discovered that it would be more than he had thought.

'Expenses like rates, taxes, electricity, gas, insurance, telephone and all the rest aren't suddenly going to drop by 50 per cent just because there's only one person living in this house instead of two,' he says. 'Having some extra money will certainly be a help to Isla, but knowing that she'll always have the support of our family is far more important.'

Thinking back to his days of working with asbestos cement in his shed, Ian says that he cannot recall seeing a single warning label on any of the products he used. Pausing for breath, he splays both hands on the dining table. 'If I'd known how dangerous asbestos was I'd never have touched it,' he says, 'even though it was such a superior product. The more that's known about this material, the better it will be for everyone.'

In February 2001 James Hardie made a strategic move. It separated the management of asbestos compensation claims from its other activities by setting up a trust – the Medical Research and Compensation Foundation – through its Australian holding company, James Hardie Industries Limited. Based on actuarial advice it commissioned at the time, Hardie established the trust with assets of $293 million.

With much fanfare, the group announced that it had established the trust to compensate asbestos victims and promote medical research into asbestos disease. The creation of the trust, Hardie said, would remove the distraction of having to manage asbestos litigation, enabling it to focus on its present business and encourage investment in the company. Hardie gave assurances that people who had been, or might be, injured by its asbestos products could expect 'proper management' of their compensation claims and that claims would be met for a 'substantial' period of time. Trade unions and groups representing asbestos victims interpreted the move very differently. Their suspicions grew as time went on.

In October that year, Hardie gained approval from the Supreme Court of New South Wales to establish a new parent company, James Hardie Industries NV, based in the Netherlands – a country where a civil judgment obtained in Australia was not enforceable. The company provided assurances that asbestos claimants would not be affected, as there was a 'lifeline' of $1.9 billion partly paid shares held by James Hardie Industries Limited in the new holding company.

In March 2003, Hardie made its next move. It separated James Hardie Industries Limited from the group (creating the ABN 60 Pty Ltd) and cancelled the $1.9 billion partly paid shares without alerting the Supreme Court of New South Wales, the New South Wales government, or the Australian Stock Exchange. Trade unions and asbestos victims' groups were convinced that the purpose of this restructure was to place Hardie's assets beyond the reach of people suffering from asbestos disease. They raised the alarm. The media got hold of the story. Governments and the community took notice, and the battle that followed was fought in the public arena. It revealed Hardie's secretive culture, its aloofness, and its contempt for the ordinary people – employees and customers – whose lives it had ruined.

James Hardie denied that the motive for restructuring and relocating its head office to the Netherlands was to avoid its asbestos liabilities. Greater international tax efficiencies were the reason, Hardie said, pointing out that an increasing proportion of its returns were coming from the United States but had to be distributed to predominantly Australian shareholders who would benefit from improved after-tax returns. What the company failed to mention was the enormous shortfall in funding of the trust it had established to compensate people injured by its asbestos products. Before long, those responsible for managing the Medical Research and Compensation Foundation warned Hardie executives that the trust could not possibly meet all future claims.

The protests of trade unions and asbestos victims' groups became so loud, and the resulting political pressure became so intense, that the New South Wales government ordered a special commission of inquiry into the Hardie trust. Counsel assisting the inquiry (John Sheahan, SC) said, 'To say that (Hardie) treated the plight of victims of James Hardie with disdain would be an understatement … it embarked upon a course doing all it could to ensure than even legitimate claims made in the interest of asbestos victims … would go unsatisfied.' He added that there was '… a culture within James Hardie management of saying whatever suits the occasion, at least where asbestos is concerned.'

In his findings, the commissioner, David Jackson, QC, said that James Hardie 'seriously misled the community' when it set up the trust. The company knew that the funds set aside were not sufficient, he said, adding that the shortfall would be $1.5 – $2 billion, and that the funds in the trust would be exhausted by the year 2007. Responding to the evidence given by James Hardie chief executive officer, Mr Peter Macdonald, the commissioner was scathing: 'A particularly unattractive feature was his unwillingness to accept personal responsibility for matters in which he was obviously personally engaged.' In his conclusions he wrote: 'There is a disturbing feature which took place leading to the February separation. It is why no one … ever appears to have said … that separation was unlikely to be successful unless the foundation was fully funded and that this was rigorously checked.'

The commissioner's report on the inquiry, released to the public on 21 September 2004, made it clear that any claims against James Hardie could not be met from the trust after 2007 unless the company were compelled to inject additional funds into it. The report received extensive media attention. Soon after its release, the premier of New South Wales urged the Hardie board of directors to sit down with trade unions and asbestos victims' groups to work out how the group would fund appropriate compensation for asbestos victims. Discussions were arduous, and pressure was brought to bear on James Hardie from all sides – from the prime minister, state premiers, the media, and from trade unions threatening a national boycott of the company's products and mass protest marches.

The haggling dragged on for eleven weeks, ending just before Christmas 2004 with an agreement – the biggest voluntary compensation offer in Australian corporate history. In the settlement James Hardie agreed to establish a new trust and provide $1.5 billion to compensate people injured by its asbestos products over a period of at least forty years. (Up to 35 cents in every dollar of the cash flow generated by James Hardie's global operations would be paid to asbestos victims.) To ensure that payments would be met during the first couple of years, even if the group proved not to be profitable, Hardie offered an additional $250 million cash buffer.

For the Australian Council of Trade Unions, the agreement marked a huge victory in its twenty-year battle against James Hardie. For former asbestos workers, the deal brought reassurance that, in the event of loss of livelihood or life, their families would be provided for. James Hardie claimed that the agreement corrected the 'unintentional underfunding' of the Medical Research and Compensation Foundation, but Australians were not fooled. They understood that Hardie had focused on success overseas while ignoring the people it had harmed in its home country.

James Hardie capitulated, but there was a long way to go before the settlement it agreed to voluntarily could be finalised. Meanwhile, many Hardie asbestos victims were left in limbo.

James Hardie brought this epic battle on itself. Establishing a trust with a huge hole in funding for asbestos claims was a move that was doomed from the start, one that caused the group to lose in the court of public opinion, the greatest loss it suffered. Unions, asbestos victims' groups, politicians and many other Australians were convinced that such a prosperous company could well afford to compensate people it had poisoned with its products. They believed that James Hardie had a moral obligation to do so and that its dogged efforts to evade its obligation were indefensible.

The scandal stigmatised James Hardie as a duplicitous corporation determined to avoid paying compensation. As a consequence, Hardie became a corporate pariah. The group's activities came under investigation by Australia's financial watchdog, the Australian Securities and Investments Commission, and James Hardie lost its chairman, chief executive officer and chief financial officer, and its corporate reputation and millions of dollars in market capitalisation.

Hardie's refusal to face reality cost it dearly. The agreement it signed in December 2004 saddled it with an onerous asbestos settlement and the establishment of a second compensation fund. If Hardie had provided adequate funding in the first place, when it created the Medical Research and Compensation Foundation, there would have been no need for another fund. What James Hardie failed to grasp was that, having lost public trust, the controversy surrounding the company would continue as long as asbestos victims remained uncertain about whether or not they would receive compensation.

Joanna Ball was born in Amsterdam in the Netherlands. After the Second World War her father wanted to get away from Europe, and he took his family to Indonesia. Joanna began primary school there and remembers Indonesia as a place where Europeans were not made to feel welcome. Given this, Joanna's father decided to uproot his family again. In 1951, Joanna and her sister Riete, aged eight and ten, arrived in Australia with their parents.

They joined Dutch relations in Collie where Joanna's father started building houses. A few years later they were on the move again – first to Narrogin, a country town further inland, and then to Fremantle. In 1963, the family moved to the north-west – to Derby, Broome, Port Hedland and, finally, Kununurra. Wherever they went, Joanna's father built asbestos cement houses for the government, as many as fourteen at a time for the State Housing Commission.

Joanna and Riete were expected to help their father. He took them to building sites after school hours and at weekends and gave them work to do. The girls cleared away the bits of asbestos strewn everywhere and held building sheets while their father cut them with a saw. Joanna describes her father as a true Dutchman – harsh and demanding, a real workaholic. She and Riete were afraid of him and did whatever he told them to do. They had no brothers, so they did the hard work boys would normally have done.

Joanna spent fifteen years in the north-west, mostly in Kununurra.

'Living in Kununurra was like being part of a big family,' she says. 'Everyone worked and played sport, you knew your neighbours, you had your friends. In the summer months the temperature didn't vary ... if it was 40 degrees at lunch time, it was still 40 degrees at midnight. We had no air conditioning, of course, just overhead fans, and I can remember sleeping with a wet towel on top of me. They say that asbestos fibres get into the lungs more easily in a hot climate, and Kununurra was a very hot place.

'Most of the people who lived in Kununurra worked for the government – for Public Works and Main Roads – but there were also quite a few cotton farmers. It was a town full of men. My father built the hotel in town for Riete and her husband to run as their own business. It was made of asbestos as well. I helped Riete in the hotel – working in the bar, the kitchen, laundry, doing housemaiding. I also helped my mother quite a bit because she had to cook and do the laundry for the teams of workmen my father brought up from Perth.

'One of the reasons my father worked so hard, I think, is that he was only allowed to bring ten pounds into Australia when we arrived from Indonesia. I don't know why that was the law, but it was the same for the other migrants ... they couldn't bring furniture or money into Australia. All they were allowed was ten pounds, so the Italians, the Yugoslavs, Germans ... they all had to work very, very hard.'

Joanna, a keen tennis player, is slender and carries herself well. Her hair is swept back from her face and her fine-boned hands show no signs of a lifetime of physical work. No one would guess from looking at this vibrant woman that she is suffering from a malignant cancer. Her litheness gives the impression of an active healthy person and her freckles conceal the pallor of her skin. But the truth is that Joanna is living with the torment of mesothelioma.

'I first saw the respiratory specialist, Peter Bremner, in 1997,' she says. 'He explained that the tumour was rubbing against the sac surrounding the lung. The friction was creating a lot of fluid, and that's what was making me breathless. I wanted a second opinion, so I went to see Professor Musk at Sir Charles Gairdner Hospital. I'll never forget what he told me. "Asbestos fibres go in and out of the bloodstream," he said, "but all it takes is for one fibre, just a tiny speck like a pinhead, to get into your lung and then, thirty or forty years later, it can activate. You've definitely got mesothelioma, but you can go on living a normal life. Just do what you want to do."'

Joanna has had fluid drained from her lung five times. A long instrument was inserted into her chest cavity to draw out the fluid, an experience she found 'terribly painful'. Each time, fluid accumulated again within six weeks. Dr Bremner suggested that she undergo pleurodesis, a procedure to keep the fluid build-up under control, but he warned her that she could have this surgery only once – either it would do the trick, or it wouldn't. Joanna went ahead with the operation, which she says was another very painful experience. The pleurodesis, she explains, involved injecting sterile talc around her lung. Once the talc absorbed moisture, it expanded and developed a glue-like consistency, helping to reduce friction and fluid build-up. The procedure was successful, and eight years later Joanna is still living. She admits to having pain, but her breathing improved markedly after the pleurodesis. Joanna is an exception among sufferers of mesothelioma, a disease which generally kills people within months of diagnosis, and Dr Bremner calls her his miracle patient.

Riete was less fortunate.

'Riete died a few weeks ago,' Joanna says, 'less than nine months after being diagnosed with meso. She didn't have much fluid at all, but she had a lot of pain. Just breathing caused her pain, and the side where the tumour was growing was so sore that she couldn't touch it. The tumour was actually growing out of her side. You could see the lump. She tried chemotherapy, but it made her terribly sick. When they suggested the same treatment for me, I refused to have it.'

Joanna has been struck by how differently mesothelioma can affect people. In some cases fluid accumulates quickly, in others there's very little fluid. Some sufferers can tolerate the pain, others find it torture. In almost all cases, the tumour keeps on growing – usually at a rapid rate – but in Joanna's case, the growth has slowed.

'What I think has helped me,' she says, 'is taking lots of vitamins every day – Vitamin C, as an anti-oxidant, and shark cartilage, which is supposed to work against cancer. I really believe the vitamins have helped me, but they haven't helped others.'

Joanna finds her situation ironic, given that her family worried for years that her husband, Denva, might contract an asbestos disease. It did not occur to any of them that it would happen to her. The reason everyone was so concerned about Denva was because he had worked underground at the Wittenoom asbestos mine when he was twenty-one. He was there for only a few months, but in that time his exposure to asbestos dust was intense. It's important to remember, Joanna says, that when talk about the dangers of asbestos started, it was always about Wittenoom. No one in her family realised that they had all been exposed to asbestos, especially in Kununurra where they had lived in asbestos houses with asbestos tailings covering their lawns. Denva was given the opportunity to participate in the Vitamin A programme run by the state government, Joanna says, because he had been exposed to asbestos at Wittenoom. It never occurred to her, or Riete, that they might also be candidates for the programme that was supposed to stave off asbestos disease. She thinks the programme must have helped her husband because he has remained healthy.

Joanna worries about her daughter, and about Riete's son. She points out that they both grew up in Kununurra and that the houses they lived in were made of asbestos, as was the school they attended. The risk for children is greater, she says, because they're closer to the ground where the asbestos dust settles. When children walk or run or play on asbestos, they disturb it and fibres rise into the air.

In 1997, the year Joanna was diagnosed with mesothelioma, her mother died at the age of eighty-six. Joanna believes that hard work caused her death. She remembers her mother as a traditional Dutch wife who never stopped working. Joanna's father, a heavy smoker, developed emphysema after his wife died and spent the last years of his life in an aged care home. He demanded a great deal of attention, Joanna says, and Riete was the one who did most of the running around for him. He died when he was ninety-three. Joanna is certain that, if doctors had investigated her father's illness further, they would have found that his exposure to asbestos had contributed to it.

Riete was a successful businesswoman, but she made time to take care of her father while he was in the home.

She was feeling unwell and suspected that she might have mesothelioma, but she did not speak of this to anyone while her father was alive. Soon after he died, Riete was diagnosed with mesothelioma.

Joanna has not yet processed a claim against James Hardie for her illness.

'No one ever told me that I had a right to claim compo,' she says, 'but some friends did say to me, "Did you put in a claim?" "What do you expect me to do," I said, "sue my father?"'

Joanna did nothing about claiming compensation until she heard from a doctor that a patient of his suffering from mesothelioma had received a payout. Joanna contacted the Asbestos Diseases Society and an appointment was made for her to see a lawyer specialising in asbestos litigation at the firm Slater & Gordon.

Tim Hammond advised Joanna that she had missed the deadline for asbestos compensation claims against James Hardie. He said he would get a barrister to take a look at her claim, however, and see what her chances were. Money does not excite Joanna, but she acknowledges that her illness has cost her financially. She lost income for about two years when she was too ill to work and has paid some medical expenses.

'I think people place too much importance on money these days,' she says. 'They'll sue for any old reason. It's just greed. The stress of my illness has affected the whole family. Money isn't going to make the stress go away or help us feel any better about what's happened.'

Riete's claim was a different story. She got in touch with the Asbestos Diseases Society as soon as she was diagnosed, and they referred her to Tim Hammond for legal advice. Riete's payout came through shortly before she died, but Joanna can see no benefit. All that matters to her is that her clever, capable sister is gone. Losing Riete has left Joanna feeling adrift.

'I kept thinking that Riete would be the same as me,' Joanna says, 'that she'd have quite a few years to live. I feel as if she's away on holidays. I can't accept that she's gone. Of course, our father didn't have any inkling about what asbestos was going to do to us. None of us did. Back then, no one realised.

'I still manage to work three days a week at the liquor store where I've been working for almost twenty years. But it's getting more difficult lifting the heavy boxes. I used to play tennis five days a week. I used to do a lot of things. Now I just do what I can. Some days I feel very, very tired, and Dr Bremner is concerned that I've lost so much weight. The pain is always there, but I just push through it all.'

James Hardie's asbestos liabilities may not be limited to Australia. Early in 2005, the office of the New South Wales Premier issued a statement saying that Hardie should be working on the issue of compensation with governments of countries where it had asbestos operations.

The greatest threat comes from the United States where litigation lawyers in the state of California are gearing up for a fight. In July 2005, the widow of a Californian worker who had been employed at Hardie's 'death factory' in Los Angeles successfully sued for compensation. Her husband had died of mesothelioma because of his exposure to asbestos, and her win against Hardie resulted in a US$250,000 compensation payout. This case marked the first successful asbestos disease claim against James Hardie outside Australia and New Zealand. It sets a precedent for what could be a spate of similar claims and presents big risks for the group.

James Hardie succeeded in achieving a high profile

in the United States and is preparing to do battle over asbestos compensation there. It has retained the services of a law firm in Washington DC with powerful political links, especially to Republicans. The Hardie strategy to deal with its asbestos liabilities in America, it seems, is to throw its weight behind the push by President George W. Bush to take asbestos litigation out of the courts.

In other countries where James Hardie has had significant operations, conditions do not favour claimants. In Indonesia Hardie has a potential liability of hundreds of millions of dollars but, as it no longer has a corporate presence there, it will make it difficult for asbestos victims to process claims.

In New Zealand Hardie manufactured asbestos products from 1939 to 1984 at its south Auckland factory where several hundred people were employed at any one time. The 'no fault' compensation system in New Zealand does not permit personal injury lawsuits, and asbestos victims receive only an 'independence allowance' amounting to about A$65 a week under a government-funded scheme administered by the Accident Compensation Commission. (On average, Australian asbestos victims receive $250,000 in lump sum compensation through the common law system.) Asbestos victims in New Zealand are fighting to bring about change, and James Hardie is maintaining its distance from the dispute. Asbestos compensation, the company says, is a matter for government.

What will happen about Hardie's overseas asbestos liabilities remains to be seen.

In Australia, the battle over the funding of asbestos compensation only caused James Hardie to falter. The company postponed finalising its December 2004 voluntary agreement for a year. The final agreement involved teams of lawyers in different countries working simultaneously around the clock, and its complexity has hindered its implementation. What is more, Hardie made the deal conditional upon receiving tax and other concessions relating to minimisation of its legal costs and a guarantee of immunity from prosecution. Hardie's conditions obstructed the implementation of the asbestos compensation deal and, by mid 2006, further delays and legal wrangling appeared inevitable.

The James Hardie group continues to grow, but it no longer stands so tall in the world. Whatever commercial success Hardie goes on to achieve, it will not be able to reclaim the standing it enjoyed for so long. In its fight to avoid paying compensation to asbestos victims, James Hardie compromised its corporate reputation. Companies, organisations of all kinds and individuals have only one reputation. Once a fine reputation has been damaged, it cannot be easily restored.

Lorraine Green was 63 years old when she received the news in February 2004 that she had mesothelioma. Four months later she went into hospital to have a lung removed.

'I spent my birthday in hospital last year,' says Lorraine, 'and the same thing happened again this year. I spent my sixty-fifth birthday in Sir Charles Gairdner Hospital.

'I'm not really sure how I got mesothelioma. The family moved into a new asbestos house in 1953, when I was 13 years old, but it wasn't big enough. My grand-father built a porch and an annex onto it. I remember him cutting the asbestos building boards and living among all that mess while he was doing those renovations.

'Later on, I married a builder. Doug had his own business and used to saw asbestos every day. I used to shake out the dust from his overalls and socks before I washed them, so I was among all that dust there as well.

Doug cut up the asbestos mainly at work, but in 1965 he did renovations on our house. In 1973 the marriage ended after thirteen years. Doug hasn't been affected at all by asbestos, even though he used it all the time. I worry about my three children, because they were among all that dust in our house as well. I've been told that it's no good them getting tested until they have symptoms. So far they're all healthy.

'I started noticing that things weren't right in the wintertime of 2003. I kept getting bronchitis and couldn't stop coughing. I just wasn't able to get over it, and when the doctor listened to me coughing, he said, "Oh, that sounds terrible." My GP sent me to Charlie Gairdner for tests and to begin with they thought it might be asthma, but then a scan revealed fluid on the lungs. The fluid was tested, and I got the news that I had mesothelioma. I was very much shocked, because I was used to the doctors telling me, "We can't find anything," and I was expecting them to say the same thing again. I didn't cry at the time because it was so much of a shock, especially as I hadn't even been to Wittenoom. I'd never even seen the place. I'd heard about different people from Wittenoom dying because of asbestos, and I also knew someone who died of mesothelioma because he'd worked on a ship. To be perfectly honest, I hadn't even thought I'd get meso, not one iota. When the doctor told me what I had, I just couldn't believe it.

'That night I went to see all my children, each one separately. I left my mother until the next day and made sure I took my sister with me. I'm not one to hide things, and it's no good doing that anyway. I'm very open. I like to say how things are. My daughter was very upset; she had a cry. My older son couldn't believe it and kept asking me for a time frame, but I couldn't give him one. My younger son had no reaction – it took him a while – but his partner was very upset. My mother seemed to take it okay, but it was harder on her than I realised.'

Lorraine used to be a tall handsome woman, but disease has radically altered her appearance. Her thick blonde hair has become white and sparse, and the creamy complexion she nurtured has a greyish hue. Her eyes are the same, but not their expression. They are beautiful, cornflower blue, the eyes of a woman who has suffered greatly and lived bravely. Lorraine is dressed for bed, in a nightdress and dressing gown, slippers and woollen socks. Her feet and ankles are tender, owing to the swelling that will not go away, and she shuffles through her living room crammed with furniture and ornaments into the kitchen. The smell of illness pervades the whole house, but it is most potent in the kitchen where an array of medicines, health supplements and associated paraphernalia stands on the counter. Lorraine clears the clutter of papers off the Formica table and sits down. The need to pause for breath makes her speech seem hesitant, but her voice is pleasing to listen to and her words are clear. Lorraine may be frail and shrunken, but living without a lung has not dulled her mind.

Lorraine was the first person in Western Australia to have a lung taken out. She believes that the surgeon who performed the operation took a big step and made history with her. Dr Alvarez, she says, had spent quite a bit of time in the United States watching what they were doing over there. She found him delightful and very easy to talk to. What he told her was that, without the surgery, she wouldn't live long. Lorraine had cancer only in the left lung. She decided to have the lung removed to give herself a little extra time and told Dr Alvarez that she was putting herself in his hands.

Lorraine was not told how much extra time she could expect. She had complete confidence in Dr Alvarez and believed him when he told her that he didn't know how long she might live. She found the uncertainty about her life expectancy easier to deal with than her children who kept pestering her to give them a time frame. They found it very frustrating not knowing how long their mother would live, but there was nothing she could say to reassure them.

Lorraine was advised before her operation that there would be side effects, in particular shortness of breath. Being short of breath all the time means that Lorraine cannot do the household chores she did for many years. Even preparing a simple meal is beyond her, and she has stopped designing and making teddy bears, a pastime that gave her great pleasure for more than forty years. Her inability to channel her creativity and to manage her life independently distresses Lorraine. She knows she's not the woman she used to be, but she is clinging to life with what strength she has left.

Depression was another side effect of the operation. A psychiatrist visited Lorraine in hospital while she was recuperating from the surgery. He told her that she was depressed, but she didn't believe him. Her thinking was that she'd been on her own for a long time and coped quite well, even though she was referred to a psychiatrist after her first marriage ended. At the time, she remembers, her nerves were really ruffled because of all the stress the divorce brought on. Lorraine married again a few years later, but the marriage didn't last long.

Lorraine's depression, the psychiatrist said, had been caused by shock. It was true, he said, that she had coped well with the difficult events in her life, but the shock of being diagnosed with mesothelioma had not caught up with her until after the operation. Lorraine continues to suffer from depression and see the psychiatrist.

'He's a lovely man,' she says. 'I can talk to him without

feeling unhappy after I've finished. He's had to sort out all my pills – sleeping tablets, medication for depression – and that's helped me feel better. All of this has been awful for my poor mother, especially as she didn't want me to have the operation in the first place. On top of all this, my brother died a few months ago because of a melanoma on his shoulder. He was only fifty-seven and his death hit my mother very hard.'

Lorraine's doctors think that anxiety has caused her dramatic weight loss, but she believes that an infection in her remaining lung was the main reason. She was hospitalised several times before the infection cleared.

She used to weigh 86 kilos and go to Weight Watchers in the hope of slimming down a bit. Now her weight stands at 51 kilos. The counsellor provided by the hospital supplies Lorraine with a vitamin-fortified drink to help her build strength. It's rather like a tasteless milk shake, Lorraine says, and she could buy it in any pharmacy, except it would cost her more. She has been advised to walk every day to exercise her muscles, but pain prevents her. The scar on her left side causes such discomfort that Lorraine can walk for only a few minutes at a time. It's a long pink scar stretching from underneath Lorraine's chest around her side and up towards her shoulder. For years Lorraine had the habit of walking for an hour each morning. She's not giving up hope that one day she'll be able to manage that again.

Drug treatments for mesothelioma made Lorraine feel so ill that she had to discontinue them.

'I've had two lots of chemotherapy which didn't make me feel too good,' she says, 'and the radiotherapy wasn't too good either. The radiotherapy made me feel really sick, it was absolutely horrible. It finished just before Christmas, and I was dreadful, just dreadful. I felt so sick they decided I couldn't tolerate it, so that was that. I had the second lot of chemo while I was in hospital. They could see what it was doing to me, so that was the end of that as well.

'I've been told that this disease just sits in your body and can come out at any time. The last time I saw Dr Alvarez he said to me, "Well, Lorraine, it's been fifteen months. You've beaten the odds." But I'm hoping for years, not months. Dr Alvarez said that in America they've got people who've gone on for twelve years after having a lung removed.

'I try to get out and enjoy myself a bit. I've got a couple of girlfriends I've known since I was six. They're divorced as well, and both of them just love me. On Saturday nights we go to a little Chinese restaurant where it's not too dear and you can help yourself. On Sundays we go to Sizzlers for lunch and make an outing of it.'

Not long after her diagnosis Lorraine made a claim for compensation against James Hardie. She contacted the Asbestos Diseases Society and an appointment was made for her to meet Tim Hammond at Slater & Gordon. Once she had made the decision to have her left lung surgically removed, Lorraine was anxious to see her claim progress quickly.

The claim went to mediation. Lorraine remembers going to the mediation room in town and being surprised that it was more like a room than a real court of law. James Hardie's lawyers argued that her disease had nothing to do with Hardie products and asked her a lot of questions. She didn't get flustered or nervous because her lawyer gave her a lot of help. He contacted Lorraine's first husband by telephone during proceedings and got confirmation from him that the building materials he'd used had, in fact, been James Hardie products. There was never any doubt about that, Lorraine says, because the supplier her ex-husband had used only sold Hardie products. Mediation lasted a day and the claim was settled out of court.

'I'm reasonably satisfied with the settlement,' says Lorraine, 'but it could never be enough to compensate for everything I've been exposed to. I've lost my freedom. I've lost my life.'

Lorraine heaves herself up and heads for the kitchen door. She opens it, and behind her house, where evidence of her illness is everywhere, is a garden full of colour. A friend takes care of the garden for Lorraine, devoting long hours to making it a place of peace, a retreat where she can rest and relax.

James Hardie was not the first Australian company to strip assets from subsidiary companies in an attempt to avoid paying asbestos compensation. Another corporate giant active in the asbestos industry, CSR, had employed this strategy before. In the early days of asbestos litigation in Australia, the tactics used by CSR to defend itself against claims made by ex-employees of its blue asbestos mine proved most effective.

PART 3

TOWN OF INFAMY

Edward Knox came from a family of Scottish tradesmen but never lived in Scotland. His father started out maintaining machinery in Edinburgh's linen mills and became a merchant in Elsinore, the Danish seaport city where Knox was born in 1819. At the age of eleven, Knox lost his father. He was an only son, with one sister, and his mother determined that he should continue his education. She borrowed money from her brother in London and sent Knox to Germany to learn the ways of the commercial world.

Five years later, speaking English, Danish, German and French with fluency and showing a flair for commerce, Knox joined his uncle's London merchant house as a junior clerk. The position proved not at all to his liking, but his uncle insisted that he serve his apprenticeship before becoming a partner. The ill feeling between the two men grew, and Knox was dismissed within a few years. In 1840 he set off for Australia intent on making his fortune.

Knox soon became bored with tending sheep on his property near Sydney and obtained a position as accountant with a real estate firm, the start of his remarkable business career. In May 1843 he became manager of an auction company, and in October that year he was appointed manager of the struggling Australasian Sugar Company. Throughout his twenties Knox made connections in business, politics, and the law in pursuit of his ambition to amass wealth. He became managing director of a banking company when he was twenty-eight and, by his mid thirties, he was ready to risk his personal fortune by investing in a business of his own. In 1855, Knox established the Colonial Sugar Refining Company Limited with only ten shareholders and the support of Sydney's most important banking and mercantile interests. CSR, as the company became known, went on to become the first large-scale manufacturing enterprise in Australia.

The importation, refining and distribution of sugar proved a fiercely competitive and unpredictable business, and Knox nearly went bankrupt more than once. What changed everything for CSR was its expansion into sugar milling in the late 1860s. Knox put his second son, Edward William Knox, in charge of the mills he built in rapid succession around eastern Australia, Queensland, in particular. E.W. Knox had worked for the company since he was seventeen and, with his father, created a hugely successful sugar business. (The eldest of the Knox sons had emigrated to Britain to practise law; the third entered the family business; the fourth became Chief Justice of New South Wales.)

A tireless worker all his life, Knox retired in 1880. He handed the day-to-day running of CSR to his son, E.W. Knox, but continued to exert influence over the company in his role as chairman. Knox was knighted in 1897, four years before his death; later his youngest son also received a knighthood. The Knox family, it would be fair to say, enjoyed a fine reputation, as did the company it founded.

One hundred and fifty years after Edward Knox took a gamble on entering the sugar industry, CSR is still going strong. Knox's son and successor drove the company with demonic energy for fifty years, boasting that its expansion 'went like an express train'. Today, CSR remains a prominent Australian corporation with intimate connections to the powerbrokers of the land.

CSR used to take pride in its history of growth and prosperity, but in recent times the company has become coy on the subject of its past. One brief but turbulent chapter mars the pages that tell of CSR's use of indentured coloured labour to clear land and cultivate sugar crops in its early years, its expansion into growing, milling, refining, and bulk handling of sugar in Australia, New Zealand, and Fiji, and its later diversification into distilleries, cattle stations, agricultural experiments, engineering, industrial chemicals, and building materials. The pages that recount the company's foray into the asbestos industry are soiled. The stains have proved stubborn, not responsive to efforts to erase them, so they remain. The chapter on asbestos describes a misguided venture ending in human calamity. It is one that CSR would rather forget.

In the 1930s, after prolonged growth in its sugar business, CSR found itself awash with liquid capital. The company had limited options for increasing its existing markets, so it looked for other businesses to get into. It took notice of the rising demand by American builders for lightweight interior wall boards and decided to start producing a similar product for the domestic market. Given the lack of soft woods in Australia, CSR experimented with a by-product of its sugar business, sugar cane fibre, and the result was its 'cane-ite' board, a product not unlike thick cardboard. In 1939, CSR started producing cane-ite wall boards for the Australian building industry.

Then the war broke out and CSR received a boost

to its sugar business. The federal government gave sugar production priority and rationed consumption in Australia so that supplies could be shipped to Britain. CSR also benefited from the government's support of other industries given strategic importance, such as industrial alcohol and building materials. For CSR, the war years were very good.

After the war was over, CSR focused on developing its building materials business. The company had already been making hard building boards with asbestos imported from South Africa and Canada and, in 1943, started producing its own supply of asbestos.

CSR operated its blue asbestos mine at Wittenoom in the Pilbara, the region of semi-desert scrub and rocky mountains in Australia's north-west corner. The mine was situated inside a hill near natural water springs and overlooking Wittenoom Gorge, a narrow ravine 12 kilometres long. CSR bought the Wittenoom mine from Lang Hancock, a local man. The asbestos that Hancock had produced since the late 1930s (using mostly Aboriginal labour) had been shipped to Britain to be used in the manufacture of gas masks. Most of the factory workers who made the masks were female, working for the war effort, and many of these women would die of asbestos disease as a result of their contact with the asbestos linings in the masks.

CSR bought the Wittenoom mine, even though it knew nothing about mining asbestos, because it wanted to eliminate its dependence on imports. It went on to manufacture a range of asbestos products: corrugated roofing, guttering, down pipes, exterior wall sheets, floor tiles, building plasters, and plaster wall boards.

Australian Blue Asbestos, a wholly owned subsidiary of CSR, managed the asbestos mine from 1943 to 1966. Operations consistently failed to comply with the state government's general health and safety standards throughout that period, but the government did not shut down the mine. The decision to close the mine was made by CSR's board of directors in Sydney; once there were no longer enough layers of asbestos left in the mine to produce a profit, in 1966, CSR pulled out of Wittenoom. The company sold the site back to Lang Hancock, but he did not restart operations. He had other mining interests, and the iron ore he produced in the Pilbara made him a rich man.

The publicity surrounding the mine's closure first alerted Australians to the dangers of asbestos, but many people believed that the reports of an 'industrial holocaust' were media sensationalism. They thought it inconceivable that such a tragedy could happen in Australia where egalitarianism was held sacred and a proud working class provided the backbone of prosperity.

It was only when the mine ceased to exist that people who had lived in Wittenoom began to learn from press reports that the air around the town had been thick with dust that could kill them. They remembered the dust well. It had been so dense that it had hovered over the town in a permanent dirty-blue haze and was such a part of their lives, always on their furniture and clothes and in their hair, that they had thought nothing of it. Now, they discovered, they could be susceptible to a fatal disease as a result of working at Wittenoom, a place enthusiastically promoted by the government of the day.

Italian migrants made up the bulk of the Wittenoom workforce. In Perth, where many Wittenoom workers settled, talk started in immigrant communities. People remembered promotional films describing how they could get ahead in Wittenoom if they worked hard. They recalled how they were lured to that tiny town in the middle of a desert by the prospect of making more money than they could earn anywhere else. They were also certain that they had been healthy when they went there, because Australian Blue Asbestos accepted only strong, fit men to work at the mine. The government had urged them to go to Wittenoom, and they had gone there in good faith. On their return to Perth, they had bought houses and businesses and forgotten about Wittenoom.

Now, it turned out, Wittenoom was such a dangerous place that anyone who had lived there could get a disease and die. At least, that was what the media reported. The government had nothing to say about Wittenoom. Why did it not reassure people that there was no cause for concern? Then there was CSR, one of the country's best-known companies. It had employed thousands of workers at the mine, yet it stayed silent. Why was that? Could it be that the government and the company had something to hide?

The early years of fighting for justice proved a bleak period for asbestos victims. CSR's aggression and intransigence frightened them, and the experiences of those who took on the company disheartened them.

In 1977, a CSR executive made the company's position on the compensation issue very clear.

'Even if they die like flies,' he wrote in a memo, 'they will never be able to pin anything on CSR.'

In the same year, CSR's subsidiary company Australian Blue Asbestos, since renamed Midalco to remove any reference to asbestos, was sued by an ex-Wittenoom employee for the first time. By then, however, Midalco was a mere shell of a company because its funds had been siphoned off. In stripping funds from Midalco, CSR had followed the example of its most important client, the Johns Manville Corporation in the United States.

Johns Manville was the biggest miner and manufacturer of asbestos in the world. In the same way that James Hardie and CSR distributed asbestos around Australia, Johns Manville puts its asbestos products into ships, aeroplanes, railway carriages, motor cars, water pipes, office buildings and houses throughout the United States.

Johns Manville showed the way when it came to fighting legal action for compensation by former asbestos workers. In Australia, CSR imitated Johns Manville and James Hardie followed CSR.

In the late 1920s, Johns Manville defended legal action by former asbestos workers for the first time. In fighting the claims of eleven plaintiffs, the company set about strengthening its position with the help of lawyers, insurers, and medical experts. It did whatever it could to thwart and delay proceedings while lobbying for legislation that would protect it against personal injury claims. What the company did not do was improve conditions at its mines and factories. Johns Manville eventually paid compensation to the plaintiffs, although considerably less than they had claimed. It also extracted an undertaking by their lawyer to take no further action against the company, a move which effectively put on hold its asbestos litigation.

This strategy adopted by Johns Manville to fight asbestos compensation claims in America served as a blueprint not only for CSR and James Hardie in Australia, but also for the asbestos industry worldwide.

Cornelius Maas was the first former Wittenoom worker to take legal action against CSR. Maas was a Dutch post-war migrant who went to Wittenoom in 1957 to get ahead in his new life. He worked in the mill for four months, and twenty years later discovered that he had developed mesothelioma. Maas had a wife and three children dependent on him and was determined to get a payout from CSR to help his family. His writ suing for damages resulting from CSR's negligence was issued on 24 June 1977. Soon afterwards, on 4 July 1977, Maas died. CSR had been preparing for a fight, but the timely death of Cornelius Maas spared the company the trouble and expense of a court case. The threat of asbestos litigation receded, and CSR appeared to have nothing to worry about.

The next ex-Wittenoom employee to take a stand against CSR was Joan Joosten. As a young woman in the early 1950s, Joosten spent three years in Wittenoom with her husband, Bert, another Dutch post-war migrant. She thought herself fortunate to get a job with Australian Blue Asbestos, working in one of the administration offices just 30 metres away from the mill where her husband was employed. Dust from the mill flew through the fly screens of the rusting tin structure that served as an office building, settling on the floor and furnishings and on the papers that Joan processed every day.

In 1979, Joosten discovered that she was dying of mesothelioma. At the time, sufferers of mesothelioma had an average of nine months to live after diagnosis, but this did not stop Joosten from suing Midalco and CSR for negligence. She was the first Wittenoom victim to live long enough to take her case to court.

Joosten lost the case and appealed. On the morning of 10 March 1980, the day her appeal was due to be heard in the Supreme Court of Western Australia, she died. Joosten's appeal died with her, but the sympathy the case aroused brought the issue of asbestos disease on to the front pages of national newspapers again. Wittenoom, the papers wrote, was a death trap.

The state government of Western Australia remained silent. It had reaped revenue from asbestos exports but done nothing to improve conditions at the Wittenoom mine. Now its insurance arm, SGIO, found itself liable to pay compensation to former Wittenoom workers if they could prove that they were unable to work because of an occupationally induced asbestos disease. The compensation entitlements were so paltry that many families affected by asbestos disease could barely get by on the payments. Nonetheless, SGIO feared a flood of claims.

CSR defended itself vigorously, maintaining that it had nothing to do with the emerging disaster. The Wittenoom mine, it pointed out, had been run from the head office of a subsidiary on the other side of the country and had been operational long ago. Besides, the company said, government authorities could have closed the mine at any time. CSR nevertheless decided to take action.

In an effort to deflect negative publicity, the company established the Wittenoom Trust to provide financial assistance and support services to ex-Wittenoom employees affected by asbestos disease and to their families. Press reports made much of the $3 million the company paid into the trust and featured stories about social outings and craft classes arranged for Wittenoom widows. By establishing the trust, CSR gained a public relations victory. By courting the media, the company succeeded in persuading Australians that the Wittenoom disaster had been an unfortunate accident.

CSR refused to accept that inhaling asbestos dust caused asbestos disease, a fact long since proved and made public in medical journals. The company went on to spend millions of dollars during its protracted battle with ex-Wittenoom employees in an attempt to disprove what had been proved beyond doubt and while the body of evidence continued to grow. Rather than acknowledge its ethical responsibility, CSR denied it.

The company spent liberally on legal services, but when it came to dealing with compensation claims from people it had injured, CSR brought its corporate might to bear. It was a wealthy company whose directors and executives ranked among the country's corporate elite, but towards its workers – men and women who had contributed to its success – CSR showed no compassion. Those who had sacrificed their lives to serve the company found their former employer to be a formidable adversary when they sought compensation.

CSR had the law on its side. All the company had to do when a former worker brought a personal injury claim against it was instruct its legal team to play for time. Western Australian legislation governing such claims favoured delay, so the company's lawyers pursued a strategy of asking for more time to gather evidence. They calculated that claimants suffering from asbestos disease would be too sick and frail to put up a fight, or that they would die before their case reached court. For more than a decade, these delay tactics worked well for CSR.

Asbestos victims were daunted by the dual battle they had to fight, against CSR and against time, and the tragic outcome of Joan Joosten's case was a blow to them. Even as she was dying, however, Joosten managed to establish a community centre to assist asbestos victims. The centre eventually evolved into a charitable organisation called the Asbestos Diseases Society. This society mounted a campaign to persuade the Western Australian government to amend the legislation governing claims for damages brought by ex-Wittenoom employees. In 1983, the government recognised the special circumstances of asbestos diseases, in particular, their lengthy latency period, and amended the legislation to accommodate people affected by them. This legislative change paved the way for asbestos injury claims to be brought forward at a time when another asbestos scandal known as the Wittenoom Papers was attracting media attention.

Joan Joosten's action against CSR was a test case. At the hearing CSR's lawyers claimed that state government records relating to Wittenoom were not available because they had been destroyed, or so they had been given to understand. Convinced that the records had been hidden, the Asbestos Diseases Society pressed the government to release them. Once they were in the public domain, the documents that had been buried in government archives for so long revealed a very different story from that presented by CSR's legal team at Joosten's hearing.

The scandal of the missing official papers changed public perceptions about why the Wittenoom asbestos disaster had happened. Suspicions arose that the government and the company had colluded to cover up the truth. Now that new and important information about Wittenoom was in the public domain, the Asbestos Diseases Society believed that the time was right for another test case.

7

Fay Noble was 19 years old and newly married when she arrived in Wittenoom in 1949. She lived there for five years.

'We left Perth in the middle of the night,' she says. 'It was winter, and I was wearing a coat and hat, boots, woollies, you name it, because it was freezing. The plane was a DC-3 – really small – and we sat on deck chairs bolted to the floor. It was a very bumpy ride, and I thought we'd never get to Wittenoom. When we finally arrived, it was three in the afternoon and 118 degrees. The pilot turned to me and said, "Would you like to come back with me?" "I think so," I said.

'Let me tell you, Wittenoom was an eye opener. It was so hot up there you had to keep drinking water all the time, otherwise you got dehydrated. The water was pumped through a pipe from the other side of Wittenoom Gorge to a big tank in the town. It was spring water, very fresh, delicious really. People just gulped it down to cope with the heat, and a lot of the blokes drank beer.'

Fay remembers Wittenoom as a very pretty place where she could see mountains, something she had not been accustomed to in Perth. The colours changed constantly across the wavy patterns of rock, she says, and, on the rare occasions when the rock turned purple, the mountains were at their most beautiful. Sometimes clouds came down low and the mountains disappeared from view, but that never lasted longer than a few hours. For Fay, the sight of those massive rocks reminded her of life beyond Wittenoom and lifted her spirits.

Wittenoom must have been one of the first cosmopolitan places in Australia, Fay thinks, because it had such a mix of nationalities – Australians, English, Scots, Polish, Yugoslavs, Dutch, Italians. There were lots of fights, of course, but it wasn't nearly as bad as some other mining towns where Aussies resented immigrants for being so hard-working, and fights got out of hand. One of the best things about Wittenoom was that people got along really well, even if they could hardly speak English.

One of Fay's chief memories of Wittenoom is getting by on little food. Shortages of food and other necessities were part of life in Wittenoom, because it was such a remote place. There were no bitumen roads into the town and, in bad weather, the trucks bringing fresh food from Perth couldn't get through. Sometimes they arrived two or three weeks late and, in the meantime, people went without. Supplies also came by sea but, when waterfront workers at Fremantle went on strike, ships couldn't leave the port. The strikes left Wittenoom residents waiting lengthy periods for goods they'd ordered – household furnishings and linen, fabrics to make clothes, children's shoes – and resentment against the port workers was rife.

The torrential rains of summer invariably caused delays in delivering supplies. In Wittenoom it never rained gently. When the sky darkened and split open, rain came pelting down, hour after hour. Great sheets of water pounded the ground, turning earth to mud and creating mayhem for traffic and pedestrians in the town. Sometimes, usually in the middle of the night, the creek flowing through Wittenoom Gorge rose above its banks and flooded the road running parallel to it. Men finishing their shift at the mine were left stranded because the company buses could not reach them. When they got home the following day, the workers found that the water pipe to the town had become blocked and people were queuing at the police station to collect water rations. At times like this, the residents of Wittenoom felt their isolation more than ever but, once the mud dried and the daily wait for water ended, tensions eased and life returned to normal.

In Wittenoom, people understood that the outside world did not care about them. They knew that they were on their own, so they managed as best they could.

Fay went to Wittenoom to work in her father-in-law's business, the mess in town. The company ran its own mess at the mine, she says, but it built a second one to provide meals to the single men when they weren't at work. There was a cool room behind the mess, and Fay's father-in-law had to buy his kerosene refrigeration from the company. In Wittenoom, nothing was free.

'We took turns working in the mess, because someone had to be there from three in the morning until ten thirty at night. The men worked shifts – morning, afternoon, and night – and I reckon we had more than a hundred men to feed after each shift. We served breakfast, lunch and dinner and made sandwiches for the men to take to work if they wanted. There were four wood stoves along one wall in the kitchen, so it got really hot in there. I must have been used to it, though, because when someone said to me one day, "Fay, it's 130 degrees in here," I wasn't that bothered. "Oh, is it?" I said.

'I used to run between the stoves to cook all the meat. I started with the chops, which took the longest time to cook, and put the sausages on the last stove. It was like a relay race, believe me. No one ever complained about the heat, and we didn't even think about air conditioning.

'When we had a bit of time on our hands, we gave the blokes a special treat – rissoles, or a cake with lots of ginger in it, because that was the only spice we had. When the rains came, or the wharfies went on strike, we really suffered. Nothing came up. We had to rely on what was left in the general store, which was run by the company. You've got no idea how expensive it was to buy food there. I can remember a time in the mess when we had nothing but spam and some pumpkins and potatoes, so we had spam rissoles, roast spam, spam pasties, and spam pies with pumpkin and potatoes. Then we ran out of potatoes, so we gave the men dried potatoes and onions instead.

'We didn't get a butcher in the town until 1952, so we just had to rely on the old spam. Even when the trucks were coming up, the fruit and vegies they brought were always pretty wilted. If you wanted nice ones, you had to order them from Perth and get them air freighted. In the summer months the government subsidised the cost of air freighting but, believe me, air freight was not as expensive as the general store.'

Fay and her husband, Ray, lived in one of the three houses attached to the mess for eighteen months. Then Ray got a job underground at the mine, and they moved into one of the family houses – 'cardboard houses' as they were known, because their interior cane-ite walls were so soft and thin. Fay remembers that the walls were so absorbent that they buckled when it rained, and that she could hear what people were saying anywhere in the house.

'In Wittenoom,' she says, 'it wasn't easy to have privacy.'

Fay had no proper furniture in her house, nothing to cover the asbestos cement floors, no fans to stir the heavy air. If she wanted rugs or linoleum for the floors, or chairs to sit on, she had to order them from Perth and wait for them to come up by ship. Second-hand furnishings were for sale in the general store, but no one liked to buy them because they were so expensive. The pub wasn't cheap either. The men were usually limited to two bottles of beer a night, four if they had a wife who didn't drink.

Ray was an experienced miner, having worked underground in gold mines around Kalgoorlie, so he was aware of the need to reduce dust. When he was in the tunnels of the Wittenoom mine, he regularly sprayed the dust with water – an activity the managers discouraged because they wanted to save water. The company did not provide Ray with a breathing mask or ear plugs. He had a torchlight strapped around his hard hat, and that was it.

It was only when Ray moved back to Kalgoorlie that he became concerned about asbestos. In Kalgoorlie he had to have a medical examination before he could work underground. The doctor who examined Ray, Dr Jim McNulty, told him to take home a phial and to bring back a sample of his sputum in it. Ray was puzzled. He'd never been asked to do this before, so he questioned it. Anyone who'd worked underground at Wittenoom was of interest to him, Dr McNulty said. Ray was surprised. Experienced miner that he was, he knew that this was not good news. When he got home, he told Fay. She felt uneasy too. 'It was the first inkling either of us had that there was a problem with asbestos.'

Fay's younger sister, Carol, arrived in Wittenoom with her parents in 1953, when she was thirteen. She went to school there for a while, and then got a job as a waitress in the town mess. Carol left Wittenoom soon after her sixteenth birthday.

The sisters come from a family of Irish Catholics and live in Mandurah, a coastal town about an hour's drive south of Perth. Looking at them at Fay's dining table drinking tea, it is difficult to detect any resemblance. Fay has an olive complexion, and her cropped hair is dark and straight. Carol is very fair, with fine fragile skin and a head of wispy curls. Although they don't look alike, Fay and Carol share the same faith. A worthwhile life, they say, must be one of honest hard work.

'It's important to remember that Wittenoom wasn't just a single men's place,' Carol says. 'There were all kinds of people there, including very young children. It was a funny old place, really. You know, when people died, they flew the doctor in. He did the autopsy in a tin shed at the airport and then jumped on the plane again. To do the autopsy, they used a couple of trestles and put a door on top of them. They laid the corpse on the door – the doctor did the autopsy to find out how the person had died – and within a couple of hours the person was buried and everyone went back to the pub for the wake. There was one time when the floods came and the doctor couldn't come, so they put the dead man in the cold room attached to the general store for a few days. It was a normal kind of thing there. No one worried about it.'

The school day began early in Wittenoom because of the heat. Children arrived about half past seven for classes and had plenty of opportunities to go swimming. Whenever the temperature climbed above 100 degrees, a company bus arrived to take the children to the rock pools of the gorge so that they could cool off. Company trucks also turned up regularly to dump asbestos tailings on the school grounds. The children liked the asbestos because it didn't burn their feet like the red dirt, and they could roll it into balls to throw at each other.

Children were safe in Wittenoom. Everyone in the town knew everyone else, and people looked out for each other. Once the children became teenagers, they could stay out after dark and walk home without a care. There was plenty for them to do: team sports, tennis and country dancing, parties, barbecues, picnics, playing the football machine in the milk bar, reading second-hand comic books in the swap shop, going to the pictures on Friday night and – the social highlight of the week – attending the dance at the town hall on Saturday night. In Wittenoom, you could have a whole lot of fun.

Fay brought three children into the world while she lived in Wittenoom: Philip, Mychelle, and Cleve. The flying doctor servicing the town, Dr Eric Saint, delivered her babies. Dr Saint later became known for his scathing reports about the levels of asbestos dust at Wittenoom and his predictions of a health disaster among the town's population.

Six months into her first pregnancy, Fay developed complications and travelled with Dr Saint to the hospital in Port Hedland, where she stayed until her baby was born. The plane was very small, Fay recalls. She and the nurse sat on a box behind the pilot and the doctor, and they had to keep their heads bent low because there was so little space.

Fay has mixed feelings about Dr Saint. As a patient she respected him and, for years, she heard people say what a wonderful doctor he was. For all that, she is very angry and upset that Dr Saint didn't warn her, when she left the hospital in Port Hedland, that her first-born child would die young if she took him back to Wittenoom.

Philip died when he was thirty-six, and Fay torments herself with the thought that, if she'd known how bad it was in Wittenoom, she might have been able to save him.

'All the mothers in Wittenoom should've been told about the asbestos dust there,' says Fay. 'Of course, if we'd known it could kill our children, we'd never have gone there.'

Fay had seven children altogether. Her four younger children never lived in Wittenoom, but they lost their eldest brother because he was born there. Since Philip died, everyone in Fay's family has been afraid that asbestos might kill someone else they love.

In 1987, several months after Philip's death, Fay thought that she might lose another son when Cleve complained of pain in his chest. The results of medical tests showed that asbestos fibres were present in his sputum. Doctors asked Cleve if he had ever worked with asbestos. No, never, he said. The whole family was afraid for Cleve, but, after further tests, doctors told him that there were no signs of asbestos disease. Cleve was put on the government-funded Vitamin A programme run by the Sir Charles Gairdner Hospital for people who have had significant asbestos exposure, and so was Mychelle. They are both healthy, Fay says, but they remain very worried about their risk of contracting an asbestos disease.

In photographs taken in Wittenoom, Philip and his friend Ross Munro are happily at play in Fay's backyard. Their sand pit is filled with asbestos, because there was no sand in Wittenoom. They are attractive children making asbestos mud pies; around their sand pit there is nothing but red earth. Dressed in cotton dungarees, the boys, intent on their pies, are smeared all over in dark-blue dust. Playing with asbestos was their favourite game. They never tired of it.

Philip left Wittenoom when he was three and a half years old, so he didn't remember it as he grew older. He led an active life and looked after his health because playing football was his passion, and he needed to be very fit. He never smoked, and he refused to become a miner like his father, saying that being underground was for rabbits. As a young married man, Philip moved to Newman, a mining town in the north-west, to work at the power station there.

In Newman Philip joined the football club. He played for the club for several years until, at one training session, he found he couldn't run all the way around the pitch. He had worked hard to keep fit, so he couldn't understand why he'd lost stamina.

Fay was living in Perth at the time, and Philip told her what had happened over the phone. 'You should see your doctor,' she said.

When Philip went back to get the results of his tests, his GP said, 'Philip, I'd rather cut my throat than tell you what I've got to tell you.'

That evening Philip rang Fay to tell her that he had mesothelioma. She persuaded him that he would receive much better medical care in Perth, so Philip left Newman with his wife and two young daughters, and set off for Perth.

In Perth, Philip was referred to the Sir Charles Gairdner Hospital for treatment. He was offered the opportunity to participate in a trial of the anti-cancer drug Interferon, although it was made clear to him that he would die anyway. He agreed to try Interferon, but he was never given it, owing to bureaucratic delays. Carol wrote a letter to the federal minister for health asking him to give Philip the chance to take Interferon and perhaps live a little longer, but in a brief reply he rejected her request. The government's excuse, Carol says, was that the drug had not been sufficiently tested on human beings, but she and Fay are convinced that the real reason for delaying the trial was cost.

'Philip's death happened very quickly,' Fay recalls. 'It

was the most devastating thing I've ever seen in my life. At the end he couldn't have weighed much more than 30 kilos.'

Carol was working as a nurse at the Sir Charles Gairdner Hospital at the time and remembers that one of the trials using Interferon started at the hospital about six months after Philip's death. One of the patients who participated was Val McKenna, a woman whom Carol had known in Wittenoom and who was suffering from mesothelioma. Carol used to visit McKenna during her meal breaks or at the end of her shifts.

'It was a mess,' she says. 'Val had a mouth full of ulcers, and she had ulcers on the soles of her feet as well. She was very, very sick. In the end she had to stop taking Interferon. A lot of the other patients on Interferon got really sick too. When I saw what it did to people, I decided that I'd never take it. If I ever get meso, I'll make my own decisions.'

Fay says, 'Philip died on 14 October 1986. All these years later, I feel almost grateful that he's the only one of my children I've lost. A few months after he passed away, his friend Ross Munro died of mesothelioma as well. Ross spent a lot of time with us in Wittenoom, because his parents were busy running the picture house in town. It was a very popular place. We used to sit outside on deck chairs and watch the latest pictures from Perth. It was always a good night out.

'Ross grew up to be a really healthy man, very athletic. He didn't smoke or drink because he had to keep fit all the time. He was a high school physical education teacher and a champion hockey player. It was a very bad time for both our families.'

Philip's widow was one of the first to receive compensation from CSR, because her husband's death was caused by asbestos exposure in Wittenoom. It was a modest five-figure sum, and she had no choice but to get a full-time job to provide for her children. Fay thinks that her daughter-in-law fared well compared with other Wittenoom widows who'd lost their husbands earlier and received no compensation from CSR. She acknowledges that the Wittenoom Trust set up by CSR did help widows in practical ways, such as by installing security screens in their homes, but points out that these women often experienced financial hardship when their husbands died. In those days there was no such thing as a Widow's Pension.

'I think CSR got off lightly,' says Fay, 'just like James Hardie now. There are elderly widows still waiting for compensation from James Hardie. Some have died waiting.'

Fay's husband, Ray, also contracted an asbestos disease as a result of his time in Wittenoom.

Ray became more and more breathless as the years went by, Fay recalls, and was diagnosed with asbestosis when he was sixty-one. He reached a point when he could no longer work, and he couldn't even walk to the letter box at the end of the garden path without gasping for breath. At times Ray became angry with himself because he was so limited in what he could do, but he managed to potter in his vegetable garden and go fishing now and then. Ray continued to live at home until, in 2001, he died of cancer of the pancreas.

Fay found losing her husband easier to bear than losing her son. She thinks that Ray's cancer was triggered in the eighteen months he spent in Japan just after the war.

'Ray was stationed near Hiroshima,' she says, 'and he saw people dying all around him because of the effects of the atomic bomb. They reckon that people were just dropping down dead on the footpath, and that anyone within a 20-mile radius of where the bomb was dropped would've been affected.

'Over the years, Ray heard about soldiers who'd been stationed with him in Japan dying of different cancers. I remember hearing many years ago, in the late 1950s, that we're all born with the potential for cancer. If you're going to get it, the cancer will attack your weakest spot. That seems quite credible to me.'

Carol says, 'I had a friend who was in Japan as an army nurse in 1946. She died of leukaemia. There are that many people who were over there at the end of the war who've died of some form of cancer.'

Fay is seventy-five and enjoys reasonable health, although she does suffer from mild shortness of breath. Her problem is not getting enough air into her left lung – somehow the air gets trapped. Her shortness of breath bothers her most when she exerts herself during yoga classes, but medical tests haven't shown that her breathing difficulties are related to her asbestos exposure in Wittenoom. 'It could be any jolly thing at all,' she says, describing the tests at the hospital as tough and comprehensive.

Fay did have a scare just before Christmas 1998, when her doctors thought that she might be showing symptoms of asbestos disease. Not wanting to spoil Christmas for her family, she kept quiet about it and, in the end, it came to nothing. She admits that if doctors had told her that she had mesothelioma, she wouldn't have been surprised, because so many of the people she knew in Wittenoom have died of asbestos diseases.

It took some time before Fay and Carol began to hear stories about mesothelioma and asbestosis. People they knew from their Wittenoom days, including a number of men who had returned to Italy, began to die in the fifties. When Fay and Carol were told the cause of death, it was usually lung cancer. It did not occur to them that these people need not have died when they did. To Fay and Carol, it was unthinkable that CSR could have deliberately put its workers in danger, and that the government had turned a blind eye to what the company was doing. But, over the years, that is exactly what they came to understand. Asbestos, they learned, killed a lot of innocent people.

'For many years we kept hearing the same thing,' says Fay. 'It was just said that all these people who'd worked in Wittenoom had died of lung cancer. In a way, that was true. Meso is a cancer of the lung, but it's different because it can only be caused by asbestos. Some of the Italians who came over for a couple of years brought their children with them to Wittenoom, and I'm sure some of those children must have died too. More children have died than adults. That's the terrible thing about Wittenoom. Now I'm seeing older people getting meso as well. They're way past the thirty-year time frame doctors talk about.'

Carol has participated in the Vitamin A programme since its inception in the early nineties. She credits the programme with helping to keep her healthy but is well aware that asbestos disease could strike her at any time. As far as Carol is concerned, anyone who ever lived in Wittenoom can get an asbestos disease. She also thinks that mesothelioma is a disease which is little understood. She believes this, because she's noticed a change in the kind of people getting mesothelioma, in particular, people who were in Wittenoom for a short time and never worked at the mine.

One person who comes to mind is the daughter of one of the town's two police officers. She attended a boarding school in Perth and visited Wittenoom during the school holidays in May and August. In holidays during the summer months she didn't come up to Wittenoom, because it was considered too hot for her, and her mother joined her in Perth. This was a girl, Carol says, who spent only a few weeks of the year in Wittenoom, but at the age of thirty-two she died of mesothelioma.

There was also a young boy. He lived at Tom Price, the nearest town, but quite a long drive away in those days. The boy must have been about 8 years old when Carol saw him at weekends in Wittenoom Gorge. His parents used to drive him all the way there so that he could go swimming in the rock pools. His exposure to asbestos must have been very fleeting, Carol says, but it killed him nevertheless. He was in his thirties when he died of mesothelioma.

Then there are all the women who've died. All they did was sweep up the asbestos dust that their husbands and children brought into the house and shake it out of their clothes before washing them. Just doing the normal everyday work they were expected to do around the house was the reason for their deaths.

Later on, in 1979, there was a different case again. In the 1950s, when Carol was living in the country, she became very friendly with a neighbour. The woman lived on a farm and helped her husband extend their house as children kept coming. She held the asbestos sheets while her husband built the rooms.

'She never smoked,' says Carol, 'and she had this wonderful talent for painting. She was really gifted. When she died of meso, it was a shame to see such waste.'

'Why wasn't the public warned about asbestos houses?' says Fay angrily. 'Why didn't Dr Saint tell any of us in Wittenoom that living in an asbestos house could kill us?'

Fay and Carol both recall how records about people who had been exposed to asbestos went missing, very conveniently. Carol cites the example of a fire at the premises of the trucking company that transported asbestos from Wittenoom to the port at Point Samson. The fire destroyed all the records relating to the Aborigines who had loaded the bags of asbestos at the mine and unloaded them on the wharves. It wasn't clear how this fire started. Once all the records were gone, however, no one could make a claim for compensation against the trucking company.

Wittenoom was a closed town. Fay and Carol were used to seeing Aborigines coming and going on trucks, but they never saw them in the town itself. Aboriginal men arrived in groups of five or six to load bags of asbestos for transport, the lowliest job at the mine. If there weren't enough bags ready at the mill, they waited outside the town until they were needed. Once they'd loaded a truck, they left with it.

The sisters also remember the saga of the missing Wittenoom Papers. For years it was said that there were 'no records, no records'. Then the Asbestos Diseases Society started kicking up a fuss in the 1980s, and the story changed. 'Surprise, surprise,' says Carol, 'all these records relating to Wittenoom were found.'

Carol has fond memories of Wittenoom as a place where she found it easy to make friends and enjoy herself. She married a miner after she left Wittenoom and lived in other mining towns all over the state. None of them offered what Wittenoom had.

'Wittenoom had its own special beauty,' she says. 'It's such a tragedy that so many people have died of asbestos diseases because they went there. Whole families have gone.'

In 1985, Slater & Gordon began its involvement in asbestos litigation. The law firm was based in Melbourne and, that year, it was successful in the case of Pilmer v. McPhersons in the Supreme Court of Victoria.

Harold Pilmer had been employed by the Melbourne hardware company, McPhersons, for most of his working life. He had been exposed to asbestos dust as a result of handling products containing asbestos fibre, such as the asbestos cement wall boards used to renovate homes. Pilmer was in his sixties when he sought damages from McPhersons, claiming that he was suffering from mesothelioma as a result of his asbestos exposure at work. He was the first worker in Australia to receive common law damages for an asbestos disease.

Pilmer's win demonstrated that it was possible for someone suffering from an occupationally induced asbestos disease to mount a successful case, even though the cause of the disease might date back many years. It also marked the beginning of the significant role that Slater & Gordon was to play in the long and bitter battle that lay ahead for asbestos victims.

In Perth, the Asbestos Diseases Society approached Slater & Gordon to assist in its efforts to bring test cases before the courts. The firm agreed to act as the society's solicitors. The first test case fought jointly by Slater & Gordon and the Asbestos Diseases Society was in 1987 in the Supreme Court of Western Australia. The plaintiff, Wally Simpson, sought damages from Midalco, claiming that he was suffering from asbestosis as a result of his exposure to hazardous dust at the Wittenoom mine where he had worked for a few years in the 1950s. After hearing evidence for more than forty days, the judge ruled that Wally Simpson did not have asbestosis as he claimed.

Losing this case was a blow to Slater & Gordon. The firm had opened a branch office in Perth and was preparing to do battle against CSR on behalf of hundreds of Wittenoom asbestos victims. Now its future in Western Australia was in doubt. The mistake that Slater & Gordon and the Asbestos Diseases Society made was to select Wally Simpson for this test case.

Simpson was illiterate and had spent his working life drifting from one casual job to another. In his evidence he was unsure of dates – for example, he could not remember in which year he had begun to experience breathing problems – and under cross-examination he gave answers that were confused and contradictory. CSR's legal team had no difficulty convincing the judge that Simpson was an unreliable witness, implying that he imagined his illness, even though he had been diagnosed with asbestosis and granted workers' compensation as a result.

Once again, CSR was the winner.

The loss of the Wally Simpson case damaged Slater & Gordon financially and dashed the hopes of people with asbestos diseases. In its aftermath, members of the Asbestos Diseases Society urged their president, Robert Vojakovic, to abandon the crusade for justice on their behalf. They believed that the odds were stacked against them and that to fight on would be futile. What chance did they have, they said, when CSR was a powerful company and they were humble migrants? Debilitated by disease and fearful of the savaging that CSR's lawyers would subject them to in court, they elected not to proceed with legal action.

Vojakovic had spent a few months in Wittenoom in the early 1960s and escaped after buying the airfare to Perth with his winnings from a game of cards. An intrepid Croatian, he had no intention of giving up the fight against CSR. Within months of the Wally Simpson case, he brought the Asbestos Diseases Society together again with Slater & Gordon to continue the battle. The next case was to prove a marathon.

In a joint case, Peter Heys and Tim Barrow claimed damages from Midalco and CSR for mesothelioma resulting from exposure to excessive levels of asbestos dust at the Wittenoom mine. Labelled the 'maxi trial' by the media, the case lasted more than eight months in the Supreme Court of Western Australia, a record in Australian legal history.

Peter Heys had been employed in Wittenoom for just two months, but in that time his exposure to blue asbestos dust had been intense – because he had worked in the mill. Tim Barrow had spent three years working as a clerk in one of the tinny administration buildings close to the mill. Thirty-odd years later, both men discovered that they had mesothelioma. Heys did not live long enough to savour his win. Barrows died weeks after the case ended in August 1988. Their victory over CSR may have seemed hollow, but it gave Wittenoom victims a boost nonetheless. They began to think that there might be hope after all.

CSR's corporate standing was sullied by the trial. Once more, the company had to confront unfavourable publicity arising from a high-profile court case involving ex-Wittenoom employees. Again, it made a strategic move. This time, CSR provided $20 million to settle what it believed to be the outstanding number of asbestos claims – those of about 200 ex-Wittenoom employees then proceeding to the courts. In making this offer of out-of-court settlements, CSR thought it could get rid of the nagging asbestos issue once and for all.

Communities affected by asbestos disease were sceptical. They knew of CSR's reputation for not giving an inch, and they doubted that the company's denial of responsibility for the Wittenoom disaster had changed substantially. In time, word got around that some asbestos sufferers were experiencing a lengthy wait to receive compensation payouts. These delays raised suspicions that the settlement was just another ruse to impress the media and pay minimum compensation to injured workers.

To be eligible for a payout, former Wittenoom employees had to prove that they were so disabled by an asbestos disease that they could not work. They had to be unemployed in order to make a claim, but much hinged on technicalities. As a result, sick people struggled on in their jobs because they were afraid of failing to meet the qualification criteria for a payout.

Former Wittenoom workers accepted out-of-court settlements that were offered by CSR, but this did not end the asbestos question for the company. Claimants kept coming. The asbestos fibre that CSR had shipped from Wittenoom and products containing the fibre continued to do harm. Years of litigation lay ahead for the company and for the workers it had employed at its asbestos mine.

Most of the young people who went to Wittenoom in the hope of making a better life for themselves were eventually affected by asbestos in some way. Their exposure to asbestos dust was intense, making it inevitable that they inhaled the carcinogenic fibres in the dust. This meant that they ran a high risk of developing an asbestos-induced disease. All of Wittenoom's residents were put at risk of asbestos disease, but most especially its children.

The strategy of denying responsibility for the Wittenoom disaster worked for CSR in the early days of asbestos litigation. Over time, however, the company found it increasingly difficult to refute the evidence linking asbestos exposure to the risk of contracting an asbestos disease, so it turned its attention to discrediting claimants and minimising payouts.

This strategy also proved successful in the short term. In the Supreme Court of Western Australia, where only a very few of the sick and dying Wittenoom victims managed to take their fight for justice, CSR's legal teams gained a fearsome reputation for intimidating and humiliating plaintiffs. Their belligerence kept asbestos victims out of the courts and slashed compensation payouts negotiated in confidence. For more than a decade, CSR mostly got its own way.

CSR's battle was to some extent defined by the size of its Wittenoom workforce – about 7000, including some who were brought directly from northern Italy. Most of the Italian recruits returned to their homeland on completion of their two-year contract and never discovered that their stint in Australia might have poisoned them. CSR knew that ex-Wittenoom workers living in Italy had no chance of bringing legal action against the company.

Once asbestos exposure had caught up with CSR's former Wittenoom workers and others who had lived near the mine to provide support services or as dependants – about 20,000 residents altogether – the company's asbestos liabilities began to diminish. By the late 1990s, more than thirty years after the mine had shut down, many of those who had lived in Wittenoom as children or young adults had died. Personal injury claims continued to be made by workers who had handled CSR building products and customers who had used them, but the company's name appeared less frequently in press reports about the asbestos tragedy as media interest in James Hardie grew.

Wittenoom was unique because it offered post-war migrants the opportunity to kick-start their lives in Australia. It was a company town where trade unionists were unwelcome, so immigrants willing to work hard were not excluded from well-paid jobs by unionised Australian workers. The newcomers went to Wittenoom to get a life. They did not know that asbestos was dangerous and that this had already been proved in a successful class action against the world's biggest asbestos company, Johns Manville in the United States. Those who could have informed the Wittenoom people about the danger – government officials, doctors, trade union leaders – told them nothing, and CSR had a vested interest in maintaining silence on the matter.

The people providing the Wittenoom workforce were desperate to succeed in Australia. For a company as rapacious as CSR, they proved easy prey. Wittenoom promised these new Australians opportunity and sacrificed them on the altar of greed.

Steve Aiberti arrived in Wittenoom just before Christmas in 1950 when he was 10 years old.

'My father had been up there almost two years,' he says. 'Before that he'd been in the war and then with the military in Perth. In Wittenoom he worked his way up the ranks to become an underground shift boss at the mine, and I can remember that he was once classified as "the best miner in Australia". He was very proud of that. He did well in Wittenoom.'

Steve's childhood had been difficult, but his life improved in Wittenoom. His father had been away for much of the time, and his mother had found it a strain raising four children on her own. But, in Wittenoom, the family was finally together, and everyone was happier.

Steve's father was an Italian who became a naturalised Australian. After the war broke out, the army sent him to work as a language interpreter at the Cowra internment camp in New South Wales, where Italian residents not holding Australian citizenship were detained. There were actually two camps at Cowra, Steve points out, one for the Italians, and the other for the Japanese. They were side by side, but separate.

Steve's paternal grandfather and two uncles were not naturalised Australians. They were interned during the war at Harvey, a country town 120 kilometres south of Perth, where they were put to work on outlying farms. They were freed when the war ended, but the bitterness they felt about their ordeal had a lasting effect on Steve's family. Today, there is a memorial in Harvey for the people interned there.

In Wittenoom, Steve completed his compulsory education, then started working at the mine as a mineral sampler. It was his job to test samples of the fibre that was ready for shipment to ensure that quality standards were met. Conditions in the mill were extremely bad, according to Steve, but there was even more dust in the laboratory where he tested the fibre. He didn't stay there long. Like all the other men, he wanted to work underground because that's where he could make the most money. He soon got what he wanted and went to work in the mine for a couple of years. In 1957, he left Wittenoom to join the navy.

The following year Steve's sister, Veronica, married Ray Mercer in Wittenoom. The Mercer family had lived in Wittenoom for years and Ray's father also worked as a shift boss at the mine. In 1960 the couple moved to Perth, shortly after Steve's mother and brothers had returned to live there. The next year Steve married Joan, a colleague in the navy. Steve's father remained in Wittenoom until the mine closed in December 1966. By then, he already knew that there was something wrong with his lungs.

'Around 1959 or 1960, workers at the Wittenoom mine began having x-rays,' Steve says. 'They had to have them, and I can remember my father's reaction when he got the report on his first one. He used an old miner's expression from the gold mines. "I'm dusted," he said. "It doesn't look good."

'The irony is that he'd given up smoking four years

before. He'd started coughing again, but he kept working hard. He was a shift boss, so he didn't do any really physical stuff. That came later, after he left.

'Once he was back in Perth, he got a job with the Shire of Gosnells putting in drainage systems. The unions complained that he worked too hard, so he was soon retrenched. He found work in the building industry putting up steel structures, but that was a real struggle for him. After three years he had to give it up. By then, he couldn't do anything any more. That was in 1971, when he found out that he had asbestosis. I didn't see much of him then because I was working all over Australia as an air traffic controller, a job I'd started in 1964 after leaving the navy.'

Steve's father was an invalid for years. He could walk only a few paces, so he sat for hours under the tree in his backyard, his favourite spot. Sometimes he got frustrated and let his Italian temper get the better of him, Steve says, but that was because of his illness. He was usually a quiet, easy-going man.

Steve's mother did not cope well with her husband's condition. She also had her youngest son, Michael, to look after, and Steve believes that taking care of both men was too much work and worry for her. Michael was a bit slow, he says, because he got meningitis when he was six months old and that left him with slight brain damage. He required a great deal of attention and his medications cost a fortune. Steve thinks that his mother must have become very lonely while looking after two invalids, and that's why she started to drink. There had been no sign of a drinking problem before then.

When Steve realised that his mother could no longer manage the situation – could not even take care of herself – he felt that he had no choice but to put his father in a nursing home.

'That was the hardest thing I've ever had to do,' he says. 'What made it worse was that the others wouldn't back me up. They simply refused to be there when I gave the news to Dad. "You've got to do it, because you're the eldest son," they said. They didn't want anything to do with it. Robert was seven years younger than me and away in the navy. Michael was nine years younger and, obviously, he couldn't do it. Veronica felt she had enough on her plate looking after her husband, because Ray was already very sick with asbestosis by then. So it was left to me to tell Dad. He took it in his stride. "Yeah, okay," he said. I think he knew in himself that he needed nursing and that his end was getting close.

'My father was not a drinker. He hardly drank at all, in fact. He smoked for a long time, but so did everyone else who'd been in the war. He appeared to handle life in the home quite well. He knew some of the other men – they'd also been in the mining industry – and he died there after eighteen months. That was in 1980, when he was 65 years old. He died of pneumonia, one of the common complications of asbestosis, and his lung had virtually collapsed.'

Steve's mother continued to drink. In particular, Steve says, she drank cough mixtures containing up to 70 per cent alcohol. One evening he received the news that his mother had 'fallen over' in someone's house and needed help straightaway. He picked her up and took her to see his doctor the next morning. The doctor told him that his mother had so much alcohol in her system that she 'should have been dead'.

'That did it,' Steve says. 'I told her she'd have to get dried out and booked her into a private psychiatric clinic for a couple of weeks. She was pretty much okay after that, considering she'd been an alcoholic for ten years.'

Steve's mother lived until 1994, when she was diagnosed with emphysema and cancer of the oesophagus, both triggered by asbestos. She was told that she'd be lucky to live six months and very lucky to last a year. Steve put her in a nursing home where she lost the will to go on and died within a week.

Steve is a very social person, but his outgoing personality got him into trouble when he was growing up. He still doesn't understand why his mother treated him the way she did, saying only that she adored her daughter and was very hard on her sons, especially him. The main problem was that he felt sorry for Michael being stuck at home so much and trying to help him angered his mother.

In Wittenoom, all the children wanted to go swimming in summer because it was the only way they could cool off. Even on the hottest days, the water in the rock pools of the gorge was always cold. When Steve went to Wittenoom Gorge for a swim, he took his younger brothers with him. They had to sneak out of the house while their mother wasn't looking, because she didn't like to lose sight of Michael. So, by the time they returned home, she was furious. She lashed out at Steve, but not at her younger sons. 'She was always belting me,' says Steve. 'Most of the time, I'd no idea why.'

Steve's good looks and popularity with girls added to his difficulties in his teenage years. On one occasion, his father knocked him unconscious and put him in Wittenoom's primitive hospital. Steve's crime had been to flirt with another man's woman. His excuse was that she wasn't married, but his father said that didn't make any difference – she belonged to the man she was living with.

In his mid sixties Steve is still handsome. A lifetime of playing sport has kept him lean and quick on his feet, and his smile is full of warmth. His cragged face is pleasingly put together, and his hair could be that of a twenty-year-old, but for a few flecks of grey. The violence that Steve was subjected to as a boy has not stunted him. His natural self-assurance attracts people now, just as it did when he was growing up in Wittenoom. In his home in a retirement village on the northern edge of Perth, there is a constant coming and going to discuss this committee meeting and that social function. Helping others is what Steve excels at. His abilities are in demand. His generous spirit and wry humour win him affection.

In Wittenoom, Steve established a friendship with Ray, his future brother-in-law. Over the years they did a lot together – football, pool, darts – and became close. Steve remembers Ray as a very kind man who was devoted to Veronica and their daughter, Lynette.

Asbestosis made Ray's life a total misery, Steve says, and he suffered terribly. Ray was only fifty-two when he died in 1986, but Steve thought it was a mercy. By then, Ray's mother and father had already died of mesothelioma, and his two brothers were also sick with asbestosis.

'Wittenoom destroyed Ray's entire family,' Steve says. 'Ray was like a brother to me, and it was dreadful to see what happened to him. When he died, Veronica was shattered. I don't think she ever got over it. She used to be a practising Catholic, but after Ray's death she became a Jehovah's Witness. That's her way of coping, I suppose.'

In 1982, when Ray was dying a slow death, Steve learned that he also had asbestosis.

'I'd been going for my regular x-rays for years,' he says, 'and whenever I asked the Chinese doctor at the chest clinic if everything was okay, he always said, "No problem." That time, I must have had some doubt in my mind because I asked my family doctor to give him a ring. He did that, then he phoned me back and told me to make an appointment to see him. When I went there, I got a shock.

'He said to me, "Do you want the good news or the bad news?"

'"Good."

'"You've got asbestosis. The bad news is that you've had it for years. The first x-ray showed it."

'"What?"

'"I asked the doctor at the clinic why he didn't tell you. He said he didn't like to give people bad news."'

Steve was not shocked by the news that he had asbestosis. He came from a mining family and accepted that working in mines was dangerous. He'd been aware that he was at risk of getting an asbestos disease for many years, so finding out that he had one didn't surprise him. What stunned Steve, and also made him very angry, was that he hadn't been told the truth. He had an incurable disease, yet doctors at the clinic he'd attended for his x-rays hadn't seen fit to tell him.

Steve was 42 years old at the time of his diagnosis. He was determined not to feel sorry for himself and to keep doing what he wanted to do. Some years later, he became one of the first people to participate in the government-sponsored Vitamin A programme. This, he firmly believes, has made all the difference to his health.

'If I hadn't been taking all those supplements,' he says, 'things would have been very different.'

He carried on for ten years, until he couldn't work any longer. In 1992, his breathing difficulties caused him so much stress that he had to give up his job supervising the training of air traffic controllers. His work was very demanding, and in the end he thought he couldn't manage the long hours and constant travel.

At the time, Steve was on the committee of the Asbestos Diseases Society and was able to get help from the society's president, Robert Vojakovic, in preparing his claim for compensation. Vojakovic had already worked with Steve on two previous claims: one for his father, and the other for Ray.

'Both those claims went in after they died,' Steve says. 'It took quite a long time for my father's to go through. Ray's was much quicker. My father had been on a disability pension, so he'd been able to manage, especially as my mother was very good with money. It was a discipline she'd learned during the war.'

Steve's battle for his own payout lasted six years.

'I went to the medical board that assesses cases of industrial diseases,' he says. 'Each of the three doctors on the board said to me, "Yes, you've got asbestosis," but that wasn't enough. "We've got to fight each case," Robert told me. "Your case must be watertight."

'What Robert said was true. CSR fought me every step of the way. All I kept hearing from their lawyers was, "Prove this, prove that." Their insurer, SGIO, sent me to see two psychologists, and Robert sent me to see a third one. SGIO brought lawyers over from Sydney and even flew a psychiatrist from Sydney to see me. It was in the middle of summer, and he was wearing a long trench coat and a big wide hat. "Have you ever thought about committing suicide?" he asked me. "Yes, sometimes," I told him. That was all he was interested in. I think he believed that I was depressed because of my family history – you know, my father and mother dying of asbestos diseases, then Ray.

'The psychologist recommended by Robert told me, "Yes, you've definitely got something," and one of the psychologists SGIO sent me to said the same thing, more or less. The other one was against me. So, it was there, in black on white, that I had a psychological problem because of the asbestosis I had and all the terrible things that had happened in my family because of asbestos.

'I was fortunate to have a very good lawyer, Luisa Formato, of Slater & Gordon. The first time she called to say that SGIO's lawyers had made me an offer, I told her what they could do with it. The offer was for $30,000, which is a lot of money to some families, especially when the breadwinner can't work any more. Later on I rang Luisa to apologise for what I'd said, but she just laughed.'

Steve had planned to retire at fifty-five and had been saving money so that he and Joan could enjoy their retirement together. After rejecting CSR's offer of compensation, he had to live on his savings while he worked on his claim. Back and forth it went, he says. There were so many little bits and pieces to do, and it all took up so much of his time. For him, and for Joan, the fight for compensation became a nightmare.

In 1998, a week before he was due to go to court, Steve attended a pre-trial conference. It was held in a mediation room at the Supreme Court, and present with Steve were his solicitor, Luisa Formato, his barrister, Mr Theo Lampropoulos, Robert Vojakovic, and Joan. At the meeting, SGIO's in-house lawyer made Steve an offer. Joan urged Steve to accept the offer, telling him that she'd had enough. He accepted on condition that all his costs were paid.

'We had a done deal before the trial,' he says. 'In the end the payout was about half a million dollars, but if I'd been able to stay on working, my superannuation would have been double that much. It's important to remember things like that. It was a reasonable payout, but no amount of money could compensate me for the loss of lifestyle.

Fighting CSR took away six years of my life, and Joan's as well. Money can't give us back those years.'

Joan is as composed as Steve is energetic, as earnest as he is jovial. She is his most ardent supporter, the stable force in his life.

'The court case was awful,' she says. 'They kept dragging it out, and I felt as if they were calling Steve a liar. Everything was there – all the medical records – but still they made us feel fraudulent. They made me so angry. It was a very emotional time, very hard. By the end, I would've accepted whatever sum they offered just to get it over with. You can only stay firm and strong for a certain length of time, then the whole thing starts to eat away at you. Steve was suffering so much under the strain of it all that I was really afraid he wouldn't last much longer.

'I felt contempt for those lawyers, even though I knew they were just doing their job. When I was sitting listening to them, I kept thinking, "You've got no idea what you're talking about."

'I tried to change my thinking – telling myself that it wasn't personal – but I did take it personally. I was angry because what happened to Steve was someone's fault. The company knew about the danger. When we watched Steve's father slipping away, it was very hard seeing all that pain and heartbreak. It seemed such a waste.'

Like Steve, Joan knew that all miners run the risk of lung disease and accepted this. What she found unacceptable was the repeated questioning of Steve's medical records by lawyers and the 'horrific things' Steve had to endure as a result.

'The thinking of CSR's lawyers was that they'd eventually get the answer they wanted if they sent Steve to enough medical experts,' Joan says. 'At the time I really thought it would be the end of him, but it's amazing how he's managed since then. Steve still pushes himself too hard. He's getting worse, but there are still more good days than bad.'

The 1990s brought more deaths in the Aiberti family.

'It was getting to the stage,' Steve says, 'when we thought, "Who's going to be next?"'

'In 1993, I got a phone call from my Uncle Ron on my mother's side of the family. I hadn't seen him in years because he lived out in the country in Narembeen. Ron had worked as a bagger in the mill at Wittenoom for only three months, but that was enough to give him mesothelioma.

'For the next eighteen months I drove Ron back and forth to Perth for all his medical tests and to make arrangements for his payout. When I was growing up, Ron was my favourite uncle. When he was dying, I did what I could to look after him and got him into a special hostel attached to Sir Charles Gairdner Hospital. Robert Vojakovic worked closely with me on Ron's payout. It came through, and Ron gave it to his children.

'The next to go was my Uncle Syd. He was also diagnosed with mesothelioma. He'd lived with us for a few years in Wittenoom where he was a truck driver. He used to drive trucks all around the mine site. It was a very dusty job, and some of that asbestos dust must have got into his lungs. Syd lived up in Port Hedland, so I hadn't seen much of him either. He'd been sick for a long time, but he didn't want to know. I went to see him in Port Hedland and did what I could to help him. He died in 1999.'

There was another death in the family in 1999. Steve's brother Robert was 52 years old and planning to retire at fifty-five. He owned a successful business in Perth selling bicycles and was saving money to travel the world after he retired. A cruise to Fiji was the first trip Robert wanted to take with his wife, but he didn't have the chance to go there or anywhere else. Within three months of being diagnosed with cancer of the pancreas, he died.

Steve remembers his younger brother as his shadow – whatever he did, Robert did too. In Wittenoom, when he went swimming or played football or whatever, Robert tagged along. When Steve left Wittenoom to join the navy, Robert followed him.

'We both got a double whammy,' Steve says. 'We were exposed to all that asbestos in Wittenoom, and then we were in the navy. Those bulkheads were just full of asbestos. Bob was in the navy for a long time, twenty-three years. Perhaps that made a difference.'

The first indication Robert had that something wasn't right, Steve recalls, was when he started having bowel problems. Robert went to see his doctor, but nothing came of it. It took Steve more than a year to persuade his brother to get a second opinion from Dr Greg Deleuil, the doctor at the Asbestos Diseases Society.

Dr Deleuil arranged a biopsy and found out straight-away what was wrong. There were blue asbestos fibres in Robert's pancreas. To this day, Steve regrets not being more forceful with his brother. He thinks that, if he'd taken him to Dr Deleuil much earlier, he might have been able to save him. Robert left behind his wife and two children, and Steve still finds it painful to think back to that sad time.

With some fondness, Steve recalls the school that he and Robert attended in Wittenoom. It had only two classrooms: one for years 1 to 3, and the other for pupils up to year 10. Steve remembers that the schoolyard was covered with asbestos tailings laid 6 inches thick. When it rained, he says, more tailings were brought in. In Steve's class there were seven pupils, three girls and four boys.

Steve was the only one to take up smoking later on, yet he is the sole survivor among the boys. Of the girls, two are still living, as far as he knows.

'Wittenoom was a poisonous place,' Steve says, 'but if someone had told us the truth about asbestos, I think people would still have worked at the mine, because they accepted that mines are dangerous. Men who worked in gold mines or coal mines knew that they were taking risks, and they made a choice. My father made that choice in Wittenoom. He was prepared to risk his own life, but he wasn't happy when I went underground. If he'd had any idea that just living in Wittenoom was dangerous, he'd never have let the family move there. I know he wouldn't have done that.'

Within a year of Robert's death, Steve saw another of his uncles die.

Emilio had been interned during the war. Unlike his brother who'd left for Italy once he was freed, Emilio had decided to stay in Australia. He'd settled in Perth where he got a job at the James Hardie factory in Welshpool. Like so many other Hardie employees, Emilio remained with the company until he retired, more than thirty years. He died of asbestosis when he was seventy-five, and Steve remembers that he couldn't do much at all for the last few years of his life.

'James Hardie was the kind of company that quietly gives small payouts,' Steve says, 'usually about $30,000. Many people who got asbestos diseases because they'd worked for the company accepted the offer they got – because they had no money. You know, when a man can't work any longer, and he can't even do all the physical work around the house and garden he used to do before, then he has to pay other people to do those jobs for him. Maybe he's getting a disability pension from the government and his financial woes are starting to snowball. So, when a company comes along and says, "We'll give you $30,000", you can understand why people just accept the offer. Besides, James Hardie isn't the kind of company you'd want to get into a fight with. They're very, very tough, real mongrels.'

In 2002, another of Steve's uncles died, this time on his mother's side of the family. Len had worked as a miner in Wittenoom for over a year and was living in Sydney when he found that he had mesothelioma. Steve brought him to Perth so that he could work on his claim for compensation with help from Robert Vojakovic. Len was seventy-six when he died, leaving behind his wife and two children. Since then, Steve has learned that Len's widow is suffering from an asbestos disease.

Wittenoom has killed several of Steve's family and ruined his health, yet he yearns for it.

'What we had up there in Wittenoom was incredible,' he says. 'It was a wild place. I had a wonderful life there, a great social life. I still love Wittenoom. I still go there on my own now and then. There's something about the place that keeps drawing me back.'

9

CSR acquired the Wittenoom mine in the hope that it could emulate Johns Manville's successful expansion into the building products industry. The deposit of blue asbestos at Wittenoom was the biggest in the world outside South Africa, but CSR was a sugar conglomerate, not a miner and miller of asbestos, and its Wittenoom venture failed. Managers did not see their careers developing in CSR's asbestos division, so they were not driven to make the mine a success.

CSR recruited senior staff for Australian Blue Asbestos directly from its sugar business rather than from outside the group, although Johns Manville managers were brought in initially to help get operations up and running. Australian Blue Asbestos had no experience of operating a mine, and for most of the twenty-three-year period of its operations at Wittenoom the company reported a loss. In effect, Australian Blue Asbestos was a mining company on paper only. The Wittenoom mine was run from CSR's head office in Sydney, where expenditure amounting to £20 or more had to be submitted for approval.

Everything at Wittenoom was ramshackle. At the mine, second-hand machinery was installed, and problems with machines breaking down plagued Australian Blue Asbestos from the start. In the town, buildings were makeshift, cobbled together in haste to accommodate the workforce. Asbestos tailings lay everywhere – on roads and pathways, on the grounds of the single men's quarters and the state and Catholic schools, on the front drive-ways and in the backyards of family houses, on the golf course, race course, and at the airport. Hanging above the town and the mine was a dark-blue pall of asbestos dust.

CSR, through its subsidiary company, Tasmania Asbestos, also mined white asbestos for a brief period during the war at Zeehan in Tasmania, but producing asbestos did not enable CSR to achieve the kind of success it had hoped for in the building materials busi-ness. In Wittenoom, CSR encountered the same problem that James Hardie faced at Baryulgil. The mining and milling of asbestos was an unfamiliar, non-core business. In the years after the war, CSR found that the asbestos fibre it produced could not compete against imports from Canada and South Africa or Hardie's domestic product.

In 1954, CSR appealed to the national Tariff Board for help. It requested a 40 per cent protection tariff on all imported asbestos fibre, a move designed to force James Hardie to rely on fibre from the Wittenoom mine. CSR proposed that local manufacturers should have to use at least 15 per cent of Australian asbestos in their products to receive tariff concessions. James Hardie fought the proposal, claiming that it would be too costly for its asbestos manufacturing businesses. Hardie won the stoush and no tariff was imposed.

Winning was not enough for James Hardie. The company retaliated by agreeing to buy asbestos fibre from CSR but at a significantly reduced price. Hardie also increased production capacity at Baryulgil and opened a new mill there in 1958. CSR proved no match for James Hardie in the building materials industry. Hardie had the vital government contracts that allowed it to exclude competitors from the market virtually at will.

The CSR asbestos mine at Wittenoom and the Hardie mine at Baryulgil had characteristics in common. Both mines existed in isolated locations, and their dusty conditions were much worse than at other mines where government and trade union representatives exerted an influence. James Hardie and CSR employed a disenfranchised workforce at their asbestos mines and successfully contrived to keep their employees ignorant about the dangers they were exposed to. Mine managers had no fear of external interference, because the outside world had no interest in what went on at Wittenoom or Baryulgil. It was only years after operations ended that Wittenoom and Baryulgil became synonymous with corporate misconduct and consequent disease and death.

Official warnings about health hazards at Wittenoom were reported to the management of Australian Blue Asbestos and to the government of Western Australia as early as 1948. Dr Eric Saint, the flying doctor servicing the region at the time, warned the company and the state government departments responsible for mines and public health that Wittenoom would produce the 'most lethal crop' of cases of asbestos disease in the world's medical literature. The letter containing this warning was one of the so-called Wittenoom Papers that mysteriously went missing among archives of the Western Australian government. It was not retrieved until almost forty years later. Warnings written in the 1960s by another flying doctor, Dr Jim McNulty, were also found among the Wittenoom Papers in 1985.

Doctors who serviced Wittenoom were caught in a dilemma. They knew that many Wittenoom employees would contract asbestos diseases, but they also understood that trying to convince workers of the danger would be fruitless given the absence of any sign of illness. What workers wanted from a doctor was a certificate stating that they were healthy, so that they could keep on working. The workers admitted to finding the dust oppressive, especially in the mill, but other than irritating their eyes, it did not affect their health. They were in Wittenoom to make money quickly and telling them that they might get a lung disease many years later would not deter them.

The state and national governments had invested in infrastructure to facilitate the development of the Wittenoom mine. Both governments were keen to see the venture flourish, so it was difficult for occupational health and safety officials to have the mine shut down on the grounds of substandard industrial hygiene. State mine inspectors regularly reported dust levels at the mine as being much too high, but the Western Australian government failed to act. This failure allowed CSR to behave as a law unto itself in Wittenoom.

It is reasonable to assume that CSR would have known from discussions with Johns Manville and other asbestos companies that there was danger to health associated with inhaling asbestos dust. What is certain is that CSR was warned in 1948 by Dr Saint about the health hazard posed by asbestos exposure and that it continued to receive reports about the danger from Dr Saint and other government medical professionals who visited Wittenoom throughout the lifespan of the mine.

Thirty years after Dr Saint's initial warning, CSR became involved in asbestos litigation. For the first decade or so of fighting compensation claims, CSR's tactics of denial of any wrongdoing, delay, and refusal to settle worked well. Once circumstances changed, that is, once the dangers of asbestos were commonly acknowledged,

CSR and its insurer, SGIO, endeavoured to pay out as little as possible to claimants. This strategy also proved effective. Not settling was the objective. Paying the bare minimum was the fall-back position.

SGIO was the insurer covering Wittenoom workers. The Western Australian government created this insurance arm to meet statutory compensation claims from government employees and to provide coverage for workers in the state's booming mining industry, an industry other insurers shied away from owing to the risks involved.

In 1988, after CSR lost the Heys and Barrows case, the much-publicised 'maxi trial', the company and its insurer reached an agreement to settle the asbestos compensation claims they believed to be outstanding. Following the settlement, CSR announced that it would never pay damages to anyone who had lived in, but not worked at, Wittenoom. The Asbestos Diseases Society again took up the fight, joining forces with Slater & Gordon and the Legal Aid Commission.

The first such victim to win damages in the early 1990s was Brent Taylor, a man who had spent the first five years of his life in Wittenoom and who contracted mesothelioma at the age of thirty-two as a result. CSR relented at the last moment in his case, paying him damages of $450,000.

A similar case followed in 1994. Vivien Olsen, a 34-year-old mother of two children, had lived in Wittenoom as a child and was dying of mesothelioma. She was awarded more than $800,000 in damages.

These cases were widely reported in the press. Once again, CSR faced a barrage of criticism over its handling of asbestos compensation claims, but the company's resolve to minimise the cost of these liabilities did not diminish. Anyone who had been a smoker, the company now said, would not receive a payout.

CSR was eventually forced to give way on the question of smokers, although it was able to exploit the medical evidence that the habit of smoking tobacco greatly increases the likelihood of contracting asbestos lung diseases. Payouts to claimants who had been smokers in Wittenoom were substantially reduced. This was significant given that most of the men who worked at Wittenoom smoked while they were there.

In July 1995, the chairman of CSR, Alan Coates, told a meeting of shareholders that CSR had settled more than 540 asbestos claims in Australia totalling more than $41 million and had more than 400 additional claims pending. In the United States, he said, CSR had resolved 2400 cases involving the Johns Manville corporation and a further 44,000 cases were pending (most of which did not involve Johns Manville).

'I think there is no doubt our share price would be much higher,' Coates said, 'if we did not have the spectre of asbestos claims over our heads.'

CSR's handling of asbestos compensation claims harmed its image. If the company had decided on a strategy of dealing with claims expediently from the start, it might have avoided the liabilities it later faced. Paradoxically, CSR never regarded its mine at Wittenoom as important. The business that delivered wealth to the company was, and still is, sugar.

Wittenoom, Tom Simcock remembers, was 'as hot as hell'. Tom worked at the mine as an underground shift boss from 1958 to 1964, and the money he saved there enabled him to buy a house in Perth. He returned to Wittenoom in 1966 but, this time, he stayed only eight months because the mine closed at the end of the year.

Now 80 years old, Tom shows no sign of infirmity. Tall and lanky, he has remained active despite the damage done to his back and knees in the tunnels of the Wittenoom mine.

Tom went to Wittenoom because he could earn more money at the asbestos mine there than at any other mine he knew of.

'I'd been working for thirteen years in gold mines at Kalgoorlie,' he says, 'but the money in Wittenoom was better because there was a tax deduction. It was called a zone allowance for working above the twenty-sixth parallel, and there were other allowances like dust money.'

The entrance to the mine, Tom recalls, looked like a black hole in the side of the hill. Inside the mine was a labyrinth of tunnels where there was so little space that men had to work bent double or in a kneeling or squatting position. The only time the miners were able to stand up straight was when they went to the crib room for their rest breaks. Every day Tom walked a mile and a half through the tunnels with his knees bent the whole time. He kept his gloved right hand on his back, palm upwards, as protection against the razor-sharp rock above him.

It was a matter of pride to the miners that their conditions were not as dusty as in the mill, Tom says. Mining was a wet process, and the use of water reduced the level of dust in the tunnels. Miners sprayed water on the rock face before they started drilling and blasting the rock with gelignite. The men working with them scraped up the ore and put it on a conveyor belt leading to the mine entrance. The ore was sprayed with water when it reached the entrance, and Tom remembers that management didn't like this at all.

'Managers kept phoning to tell us to turn off the water,' he says. 'They didn't want us to spray. When they did that, I turned up the tap.'

The ore was crushed in a tin shed near the mine before

being sent down the hill to the mill. The fibre had to be completely dry before it could be packed, and in the mill wood fires were used for the drying process. Once it was ascertained that the fibre met quality standards, the end product was ready for transport.

'The mill really was the worst place to work,' Tom recalls. 'They used those wood fires, but there was no extractor to take out all the dust that the drying process created, and the heat was unbearable. The bagging section was the worst. Those men had to stand on a ramp to pack the fibre, and they were surrounded by so much dust that you couldn't see their upper bodies, just their legs. When mine workers played up, we threatened them with a fortnight in the mill. That usually did the trick.

'The men who worked in the mine were damn good fellows. Most of them – I'd say 65 to 70 per cent – were Italians. There were desperate to work in the mine, but they weren't allowed to until they learned to read the signs and communicate. They were willing to work and they were well paid. Men wanted to do double shifts – the more dirt they shovelled, the more money they made. As a general rule, workers would do a day shift one week and a night shift the next. This system was regarded as fair. In all the time I was there I never lost a man, though fatalities did occur at the mine.'

Tom describes Wittenoom as a competitive place where most people went for the money. Competitions to see who could shovel asbestos tailings into a drum the fastest were popular events in the town and, at the mine, the men who worked hardest and earned the most money received recognition from the company. Not all of the men were disciplined, however, and some frittered away their earnings in the betting shop and the pub.

According to Tom, there was quite a bit of snobbery in Wittenoom. In the managers' residential compound near the mine, the senior managers had the houses on the highest ground, at the foot of the hill, and their subordinates lived lower down. Managers socialised separately from the workers, and at the mine they let the shift bosses and supervisors deal with them.

Tom had little patience with the pretentiousness of some of the managers, in particular, 'the freemasonry factor', as it was called. In his view, the senior staff members who were freemasons fostered a culture of secretiveness and petty rivalry among the management of Australian Blue Asbestos, to the detriment of everyone working at the mine.

Today, Tom is thankful to be alive and relatively unscathed by Wittenoom.

'I count myself lucky,' he says. 'So many of the men I knew in Wittenoom have died, but I'm still here. I've only got 10 per cent asbestosis. Mind you, I feel as if I've had it for fifty years.

'When it comes to trying to get compensation for what's happened, CSR has been against us all the way. A lot of the men who worked in Wittenoom suffer from arthritis and rheumatism, but there's no way they could claim compensation for these conditions even if they can hardly walk. There's just no way.'

10

Many of the migrants who went to Wittenoom grew up on farms near Vasto on Italy's central Adriatic coast. In the winter of 1944, German forces brought terror to Vasto when they occupied the city on their two-year retreat from the Italian peninsula. Soldiers ransacked shops, homes and farms in a desperate search for food, forcing the local population to go without. They commandeered men to dig trenches, cut down trees, and do other hard labour, and they attacked people at random in their drunken rampages. Any Vasto man who shot a soldier had to watch the slaughter of his family before he was killed.

Vasto's ordeal continued for months until Allied fighter planes won the battle of the skies. On the ground, the Germans retreated north and Allied forces arrived. By the time it was all over, Vasto had nothing left to offer its population.

In the years after the war, the young men of Vasto left in large numbers to work abroad on farms, in factories, and in mines. They emigrated mainly to Australia, Canada, and South Africa to escape poverty, to support their families, and to avoid military service in some cases. The eldest son in a family was usually the first to leave, and he was often expected to help his unmarried sisters by paying their fare from Italy and finding a suitable husband for them. Some of these men never saw their parents again. Others struggled for years so that their families could join them.

Most of the Vasto men who came to Australia settled in Perth. They worked hard and made sacrifices to get ahead and, within their close community, word soon got around about the astonishing amount of money to be made at the Wittenoom mine.

The migrants came from a farming community where owning property meant everything, but they left Vasto with nothing but their personal belongings. In Perth they wanted what everyone else aspired to – a home of their own on a block of land. It was natural that some of these young men fell in love, but to be with the girl they loved they had to marry her. There was no other way, and it was not uncommon for a man to be told by his future father-in-law that he had to buy a house before the wedding. No house, no wife – that was how it was. Wittenoom promised these men the opportunity to buy a house quickly. It was a promise many of them could not resist.

The 1500-kilometre flight from Perth to Wittenoom arrived at the hottest time of the day. Stepping onto the melting tarmac, the men from Vasto felt their faces redden as the thick heat engulfed them. It was a short walk to the tin shed ahead of them, but sweat was trickling down their necks by the time they reached it. In the shed, they collected their suitcases and received instructions from a company representative to board the bus parked outside.

On the twenty-minute trip into town, they encountered a landscape like no other they had seen. The sky above them was distant and dazzling blue, the plain before them rust-red and immense. Green and yellow grasses and mauve mulla mulla flowers grew out of the parched earth, and ribbons of red dust drifted lazily through the air. Rising from the plain were mountains of rock, gigantic boulders glinting pink, purple, grey and brown under the blazing sun. Gazing at this glory through the dusty windows of the bus, the men were mesmerised. This was a place of rare and spectacular beauty where everything moved in the heat.

In Wittenoom, the buildings along the main street were made of concrete slab. A hill overlooked the street, and on it stood the asbestos tank containing the town's water supply. The men drove through the main street and passed the hotel before they got off the bus. At the entrance to the single men's residential compound, they saw the ablution block with its outdoor showers and cement washing troughs, and behind it stretched rows of identical tin shacks, not unlike the garden sheds in which some of the men had been living. Each shack had four foldable beds, with a steel wardrobe alongside, rough timber shutters in the window frames and doorways, and no shade whatsoever.

Workers with families were also accommodated in the town, in the 'cardboard houses', where the interior walls, made from sugar cane fibre, swelled with moisture in the wet season. The houses had tiny rooms, concrete floors throughout, and a wood-fired oven in the kitchen. Space was so scarce that families gathered on the verandah at meal times, sitting at a rectangular table on dynamite boxes rather than on chairs.

Managers lived 12 kilometres out of town, at the other end of Wittenoom Gorge. Their residential compound was shaded by tamarisk trees and oleander bushes, and it faced the slagheap at the foot of the hill in which the mine was located. The houses were well spaced, and had deep wooden verandahs and neat green lawns. Nearby, within easy walking distance for the children, lay the rock pools of the gorge.

Managers' wives did not take in lodgers, but other married women did. In kitchens, where the temperature frequently climbed above 40 degrees, they prepared three meals a day for their families and for the single men who paid for their home-cooked food. The canteens in Wittenoom offered traditional Australian fare – such as beef or lamb served with boiled potatoes and vegetables, followed by pudding – but the European migrants, the Italians in particular, preferred pasta with chicken or veal, a garden salad, and fresh fruit for dessert.

The women who cooked for single men also gave them sandwiches to take to work. Some housewives used the cheapest bread they could buy and filled their sandwiches with slices of apple; others bought fresh crusty bread from the local baker and were generous with their fillings of salami and cheese. Supplies in Wittenoom were limited, so many housewives ordered dried and tinned foods from grocers in Perth. The truck supplying Wittenoom's general store pulled into the main street once a week, and the 'special order truck' arrived once a fortnight.

Lodgers usually slept on a concrete verandah behind a sheet of canvas. If several lodgers lived in a house, they took it in turns to sleep, depending on their working hours at the mine. The housewives who looked after them washed their laundry in a steel drum with a heating element supplied by the company. The men's work clothes were stiff with asbestos dust, and their sheets and towels were stained by the red dust that settled on everything. Some women asked their husbands to buy them a second-hand washing machine at the general store to make their work easier.

Wittenoom was full of single men, but any man who

attempted to seduce a girl was likely to be driven out of town. Some of the wives took a lover, but most of the unmarried men in Wittenoom had no intimate contact with women while they lived there.

At the Perth recruitment office of Australian Blue Asbestos, men applying for a job at the Wittenoom mine found that they would have to pass a physical examination if they wanted to work there.

'We take only very fit strong men,' the recruitment officer told them. In Perth, the men heard that the more asbestos ore they shovelled in the mine, the more money they would earn.

In Wittenoom, new arrivals learned that they could not work in the mine until they had done a six-month stint in the mill at a much lower rate of pay. They had no choice but to stay. The company had paid for their airfare to Wittenoom, and they could not leave until they had repaid the debt.

The mill, the men soon discovered, was an inferno of heat and dust. It was housed in a corrugated-iron building with poor ventilation and no windows. The heat had nowhere to go, so temperatures soared, and sweat poured off the workers. The lumpish asbestos fibre came down chutes into the mill to be packed for transport. Standing below the chutes, workers grabbed the fibre, dropped it into open bags and compressed it with sticks of wood. They were required to wear breathing masks, but the dust was so dense and sticky that it blocked the filters within minutes. The workers had to keep taking off their masks to clean them, but they could not fight the dust. It got into their nostrils and mouths and settled on their clothing, skin and hair.

'Oh, here come the grey ghosts,' people said, when mill workers returned to town.

Conditions in the mine were also terrible. The tunnels had been opened up as low as possible so as not to waste any more asbestos than was necessary. They were about as high as a kitchen table, 90 millimetres or so, and miners could never stand up straight while they worked. To move through a tunnel, men often crawled on all fours or wriggled along on their backs to avoid being gashed by the jagged rock hanging from the roof; and to go from one tunnel to another, they climbed up and down long steel ladders. At the end of a shift, it took the men a minute or two to ease the stiffness in their backs, but they were young and strong and thought nothing of it.

There were three work shifts at the mine – from eight in the morning until four in the afternoon; from four in the afternoon until midnight; and from midnight until eight the next morning. Company buses drove workers back and forth between the mine and the town, through the gum trees and the sheer rock walls of the gorge. After work, the men gathered at the pub before eating in one of the canteens or with a family.

In Wittenoom, friendships were important, because life was hard, and people needed each other. The Vasto migrants who returned to settle in Perth continued the friendships they had formed in Wittenoom, sometimes for decades. They saw each other regularly at their social club where they lost one member after another to asbestos disease over the years.

By the late 1980s, asbestos disease had become the main topic of conversation among many of the club members who had worked in Wittenoom. On Saturday nights, they lingered at tables near the dance floor to discuss this one who was feeling sick and that one who had died.

Lorenzo Chiera grew up near Vasto. He was one of seven children, the first son, and when he turned fifteen, he left school to work on his father's farm. In 1956, Lorenzo travelled to Australia. He was eighteen when he arrived in Perth and, within a few days, he found a job in a plaster factory. Three years later, he met a girl at a dance and fell in love with her. The next week he proposed marriage. His proposal was accepted by the girl's father on condition that he bought a house before the wedding. A month later, in November 1959, Lorenzo went to Wittenoom. He worked there for two years, first in the mill for about six months, then at the mine. His sacrifice in Wittenoom enabled him to buy a house in Perth where he and his wife would later raise their three sons.

Lorenzo first became aware that asbestos might be harmful to his health after the Wittenoom mine closed in 1966. He was twenty-eight at the time, a physically powerful man in his prime. His strength and fitness made him employable, and he took pride in his body. He never smoked, drank little alcohol, and went to the beach for a run several times a week. Fishing and gardening were his favourite pastimes, and in summer he went for a swim after his run. Even though he understood that the dust he had inhaled at Wittenoom could kill him, Lorenzo thought that nothing would happen to him because he looked after himself so well.

In the late 1970s, Lorenzo's understanding of the dangers of asbestos increased when ex-Wittenoom employees began to sue CSR for damages. By the late eighties, the dangers of asbestos were well known not only among members of the mining workforce but also among the wider Australian public. For his part, Lorenzo was watching his Wittenoom friends die one by one. In May 1989, he learned from a respiratory specialist that his lungs were inflamed and that asbestos bodies were present in them. This news devastated him. He feared that the presence of asbestos fibres in his lungs meant that he had an asbestos disease, even though the specialist had assured him that there was no evidence of it. At the time, Lorenzo's best friend, Giuseppe, who had worked with him in Wittenoom, had been diagnosed with mesothelioma.

For years Lorenzo had been trying to tell himself that his friends were dying because they were heavy smokers or drinkers, but when Giuseppe was diagnosed with mesothelioma, Lorenzo had to search for another explanation. Giuseppe did not smoke or drink, but he had breathed in a lot of dust when he worked as a plasterer. Watching Giuseppe die of mesothelioma convinced Lorenzo that plaster dust was damaging to the lungs. He decided that he had to leave the factory where he had worked for more than thirty years because it was full of plaster dust.

At fifty-one, Lorenzo was a foreman, the highest position he could attain at the factory. He was saving to retire at sixty, but observing his best friend suffering from mesothelioma – brought on, he felt certain, by inhaling plaster dust as well as asbestos fibres – distressed and alarmed him so much that he handed in his resignation.

In Lorenzo's mind, there was a connection between exposure to plaster dust and the risk of contracting mesothelioma. His family doctor assured him that plaster dust would do him no harm, but Lorenzo did not believe him. Any kind of dust, he thought, would be bad for his lungs. He gave three months' notice, enough time to train someone to take his place, and left the factory in October 1989. In cutting short his career, Lorenzo forfeited a large portion of the superannuation benefits he had been counting on for his retirement.

He found a job as a public parks attendant, cleaning up debris and doing minor maintenance work. He thought that being out in the fresh air would do him good; instead he became tired and breathless and began to suffer from pain in his chest. Convinced that he had an asbestos disease, he went to see his family doctor on several occasions. At each visit, his doctor told him that there was nothing wrong with him. The more Lorenzo worried, the more listless and despondent he became. He slept poorly, and in the mornings he often felt so sad that he shed tears. At the end of 1990, he was referred to Dr Ian Baker, a psychiatrist.

Dr Baker first saw Lorenzo early in 1991. He told him that he was suffering from severe depression, a disease which had nothing to do with his fears about asbestos. It was his view, Dr Baker said, that Lorenzo had been suffering from depression for about ten years, although he might not have been aware of it. He believed that Lorenzo's depression had occurred spontaneously, as was often the case, and could be treated with medication. Depressive illnesses often ran in families, Dr Baker said, before asking Lorenzo if he could remember anyone in his family who had suffered from depression.

Lorenzo replied that his parents, brother and five sisters were all healthy and living in Perth, and that no one in his family had ever been depressed. He spoke of his sadness after the death of his eldest son in 1980, but Dr Baker said that he seemed to have handled this loss quite well – much better than he was coping with his fears about asbestos – and that this trauma had not brought on his illness.

Lorenzo insisted that his depression had been triggered by the deaths of his friends and the deterioration in his own health. He was certain that his body was telling him that he was dying, and that his shortness of breath, fatigue and pain were symptoms of an asbestos disease. The idea that his depression was in no way connected to his asbestos experience confounded Lorenzo. Dr Baker reiterated his view during subsequent sessions, but Lorenzo rejected it.

He took the medications prescribed by Dr Baker, but complained that they made him 'feel like a zombie'. After several months, he could no longer afford Dr Baker's fees and obtained a referral to consult another psychiatrist, a younger doctor who bulk-billed Medicare for his professional fees.

Lorenzo started seeing Dr Lars Johansen late in 1991. Dr Johansen confirmed that he was suffering from severe depression, but agreed that his fears and anxieties about asbestos had triggered it. He tried various drugs to help Lorenzo get better, but a year passed, then another, before he achieved a modest improvement.

Meanwhile, Lorenzo's physical symptoms were worsening, but x-rays revealed nothing wrong, just a little fluid on the lungs sometimes. Then, one Sunday morning in October 1993, Lorenzo felt that he could not breathe at all. He went to the emergency ward of the Sir Charles Gairdner Hospital where doctors said that he had atypical pneumonia and prescribed antibiotic drugs.

Lorenzo took the medication for six months, but his pain intensified. He could not sleep, or even turn over in bed, and during the day he dragged himself around. Doctors urged him to pull himself together and go back to work. 'How can I work when I can't breathe?' he said. By March 1994, he was in agony. He disputed the diagnosis of atypical pneumonia and asked to have fluid taken from his lungs and tested. A few days later, he received a telephone call from the hospital telling him to come in to be admitted for a lung biopsy.

Lorenzo's dread of asbestos disease turned out to be a self-fulfilling prophecy. Results of the biopsy revealed that he had mesothelioma and as little as six months to live.

Until 1994, personal injury claims made by asbestos victims against former employers were for physical disease and disablement, loss of life, loss of past and future earnings, the costs of medical and palliative care, and the like. Then came Lorenzo's case in which he sued CSR and Midalco for his depression, a psychiatric injury, as well as for developing mesothelioma.

In an expedited case brought before the Supreme Court of Western Australia in August 1994, Lorenzo sought to prove that seeing his friends die of asbestos disease and his fear that he would inevitably meet the same fate had caused his depression.

Dr Baker was called as an expert witness for the defence in the case. In his testimony he described Lorenzo's obsession with the issue of asbestos:

'His attribution of his illness to the whole question of asbestos was so strong that, however effective the treatment, it was going to be very difficult to persuade him to relinquish his symptoms. It's common to see things that have happened in a person's life mixed up with the symptoms of illness, and it's easy to assume that those experiences contributed to the illness, but that isn't necessarily the case. Sometimes an illness comes on spontaneously, but it occurs, of course, in a person who has a particular set of memories and experiences. The essence in this case is whether the experiences at Wittenoom were simply unpleasant memories and worries that arose when his depression came on spontaneously, or whether these experiences triggered his illness.'

On the subject of Lorenzo's decision to leave the factory, Dr Baker had this to say:

'He had a definite, though somewhat unsophisticated, view that the way he was feeling was purely the result of his breathlessness and his worries about his lungs, and that the situation would improve if he left the plaster factory. He believed this, even though he'd been told that plaster dust does not cause asbestos disease. Unfortunately, this is the sad sort of thing people do when they're depressed. They think that the situation will improve if they change jobs or houses, or even husbands or wives. Sadly, it usually does not.'

The judge, Justice Paul Seaman, wanted to know if it was possible for anyone to have a very good understanding of depressive illnesses. Well, Dr Baker told him, some people understood depression better than others, but someone of Lorenzo's ethnic background did not have the understanding that a person from a different background would have.

Appearing as an expert witness for the plaintiff, Dr Johansen testified for several hours as the lawyers battled over the question of what had caused Lorenzo's depression. Had his asbestos anxieties, grief and uncertainty triggered it? Or had it been an existing illness going back about ten years, as Dr Baker maintained?

In his testimony, Dr Johansen gave his views about Lorenzo's fear of dust and tobacco smoke and the traumatic stress he had suffered:

'When he discovered that asbestos disease was caused by asbestos fibres, this knowledge, coupled with later observations that his peers from Wittenoom were dying even if they were non-smokers, created a great deal of anxiety in him. He became so scared of dusty conditions and people who smoked that he avoided them. His knowledge that working in Wittenoom was associated with lung disease, cancer and death was a traumatic situation for him, and his perception that the factory where he worked was very dusty was also traumatic. He was worried that the dust would affect his lungs, and his anxiety caused him to leave the factory. In my opinion, his exposure to asbestos in Wittenoom contributed to his depression. Sometimes, depression can be an early feature of cancer.'

The crucial question Justice Seaman had to answer about Lorenzo's depression was this: Did Lorenzo's understanding of the Wittenoom tragedy, gained from the media and his circle of friends, trigger his depression?

The judge also had to make a decision about the timing of Lorenzo's illness. When did he first become depressed? Was it in 1989, when he discovered that he had an asbestos-induced inflammation of his lungs? Or was it much earlier, about 1980, as Dr Baker believed?

Justice Seaman was solicitous in his manner towards Lorenzo throughout the three-day hearing and ensured that the defence had no opportunity for bull-terrier tactics when cross-examining him. He would usually have taken a couple of weeks to prepare his judgment, but in view of Lorenzo's very short life expectancy, he worked over a weekend to deliver his judgment orally a few days after the hearing.

In handing down his judgment, Justice Seaman referred to Lorenzo's affable personality and physical well-being before he suffered depression, his love of the outdoors and devotion to his family, his description of the appalling working conditions at the Wittenoom mine, his increasing fear that he would contract an asbestos disease, and the despair he felt in 1989 when he learned that he had asbestos fibres in his lung. 'This big shock really killed him,' the judge said, 'and he had feelings of hopelessness and panic.'

He raised the death of Lorenzo's best friend and noted how this event coincided with the dramatic change in Lorenzo's behaviour and his decision to leave his long-term employer: 'It strikes me as extraordinary for a man of the plaintiff's background and attributes to give up a well-paid, responsible job as a foreman with a company in which he was highly respected – unless he was driven to it by some particular factor.'

In drawing legal conclusions from his findings, Justice Seaman said, 'It seems to me that ... two years of exposure to asbestos dust in Wittenoom caused the plaintiff's depressive illness.' He went on to say, 'He would never have suffered this depressive illness if he had not worked in asbestos dust in Wittenoom.'

In finding CSR and Midalco liable for Lorenzo's psychiatric injury, the judge said, 'In my opinion, psychiatric illness engendered in that way should have been foreseen by a reasonable employer.'

Justice Seaman awarded Lorenzo general damages for his pain, suffering and loss of life caused by mesothelioma, noting that it was one of the worst cancers afflicting human beings ending invariably in a terrible death.

He also awarded Lorenzo general damages for his psychiatric illness, saying that it had been severe from the time he left the factory in October 1989 until the diagnosis of mesothelioma in March 1994. He described this period when Lorenzo's physical and mental health collapsed as 'a very long time of misery and unhappiness and fear'.

Lorenzo was the first asbestos victim in Australia to succeed in claiming compensation not only for a physical disease resulting from asbestos exposure at a workplace, but also for a psychiatric illness arising from the fear of contracting such a disease.

By the time Lorenzo testified in court, his tumour had grown so large that a lump the size of a melon protruded from his back, his voice was so feeble that it kept fading away, and his pain forced him to take rest breaks throughout his testimony.

For asbestos victims Lorenzo's win marked a milestone in their struggle for justice, but this landmark court case did not lead to a flood of claims for psychological suffering by ex-Wittenoom workers, as might have been expected. Proving the causes of depression in court is a daunting challenge for anyone, and only the bravest can win a legal battle when they are about to die.

Lorenzo died soon after his hearing, in November 1994.

Vasto, the place where so many Wittenoom workers came from, still struggles to maintain its population. Its sports field is strewn with debris, its public library languishes in dinginess, and throughout the miserable damp of winter people huddle indoors. In summer, the city comes alive when holidaymakers from northern Europe swarm its beaches, bars, shops and restaurants. Once the tourists leave, businesses are boarded up and quiet returns to the streets and the seaside. Three times a day, a bus destined for Rome takes the young and the talented away from Vasto. Like the thousands who left after the war, these people believe that their lives elsewhere will be better. Their journey takes them through mountainous terrain, past the ruins of solitary stone forts and villages, onward to places offering opportunity. Some of the travellers make their way to Perth, a sister city of Vasto since 1989.

Wittenoom, the place where so many Vasto migrants hoped to better themselves, lies in tatters. It was a temporary town erected to service the mine and has not withstood the vicious winds and torrential rains that assault it annually. The tons of mine residue dumped in and around Wittenoom are there to stay, and rust and decay are everywhere. The concrete buildings are gone, as are the cardboard houses, the rows of shacks, the cinema and the boisterous hotel. At the other end of Wittenoom Gorge, the mouth of the disused mine gapes open in the hillside and the slagheap towers over the remnants of the managers' houses.

The magic mineral town beckoned to those who put their faith in discipline and hard work. The people who went there had high hopes, but many were doomed as soon as they arrived. Wittenoom's betrayal of its people has made it a town of infamy, but there are those who treasure fond memories of it. Wittenoom has caused calamity, yet inspired affection. It is a post-war phenomenon we cannot entirely explain.

Wittenoom contaminated itself with so much toxic waste that it can never recover. Like so many remote communities throughout the harsh hinterland of Australia, this town was destined to have its moment before sinking into the desert. Wittenoom lost its reason for existence long ago, and what remains of it will soon surrender to the rust-red earth.

PART 4

BAD HATCHES

11

Perth's port at Fremantle was a large handling facility for asbestos cargo. Imports arrived for use in local industries, predominantly James Hardie's cement factories in Perth, and for onward shipping to other Australian ports. The blue asbestos fibre produced in Wittenoom came by ship from Point Samson for delivery to the Hardie plants and for shipment to eastern Australia and export markets. In the mid 1960s, the peak period of asbestos consumption in Australia, tally clerks at Fremantle port counted about 3000 tons of blue asbestos fibre coming off ships every week.

Loading or unloading the asbestos cargo on a vessel could take several weeks. The airless hulls filled with asbestos dust, and the men lifting and stacking the bags of fibre unwittingly put their lives at risk. Workers handling the bags on the quayside also inhaled asbestos dust as it rose from the ships' holds and blew around them.

Fremantle waterside workers were exposed to asbestos for most of the twentieth century, but their exposure was greatest from the 1940s to the 1970s, when construction activity created the demand for asbestos fibre.

Rosalie Evans has been the office manager of the Fremantle branch of the Maritime Union of Australia since the late

1980s. An intelligent and vivacious woman, she has co-ordinated the union's efforts to help waterfront workers affected by asbestos disease.

'We've been struck so hard by asbestos,' she says. 'I can remember attending Christmas functions where there were three or four hundred wharfies and thinking to myself, Every single one of these guys could die of an asbestos disease.

'It was true. All of those men had worked with asbestos, and the danger was real. I think there'd be very few industries where you could say that *all* the workers were exposed to asbestos and could die as a consequence of that. That's why it's such a tragedy for the wharfies.'

What strikes Rosalie is that so many of the men she has seen destroyed by asbestos were exceptionally fit and strong. Some of them, she says, were athletes playing in the top level of Western Australian football in the 1950s. They lived by the motto, 'My body is my temple', and they kept fit all their lives until *bang* they were diagnosed with mesothelioma. In a cruel irony, Rosalie thinks, the more effort a man made to keep fit and healthy, the more likely he was to get an asbestos disease.

'It's extraordinary,' she says. 'I've never been able to understand it. I mean, how can we explain how some people get it and others don't?'

For Rosalie, the saddest thing of all is that men have died needlessly. There was knowledge that asbestos was harmful, she says, but whenever waterfront workers complained about the asbestos dust being so thick in the holds, their foremen mocked them. 'Oh, don't carry on,' they used to say, 'asbestos is so safe you can eat the stuff.' The foremen didn't know any better themselves, Rosalie points out. They were just repeating what they'd been told 'from above' by their employers.

Rosalie believes that people have forgotten how vigorously asbestos was promoted in Australia. Asbestos was all around her, she remembers, when she was growing up in the fifties and sixties. In the early 1970s, when she got married, one of the first things her mother gave her was an asbestos mat for the stove. The mats were very common at the time, Rosalie recalls, because it was difficult to control heat on the cook tops that people had back then. If a housewife was heating milk, for example, she didn't want it to boil over, so she put an asbestos mat under the saucepan. In those days, owning an asbestos house was considered desirable, Rosalie says, and people who bought one got cheaper insurance, because asbestos was supposed to be fireproof. But Rosalie suspects that the real reason for the discounted insurance was that insurers had close links to asbestos companies like James Hardie.

It is Rosalie's view that the pre-shrunk asbestos fibre imported from Canada did great damage to Fremantle waterfront workers.

'It was coarse corrugated white fibre produced by Johns Manville for pipe insulation,' she says, 'and I'm sure that the number of victims from that product alone has been huge. Then, of course, there was all the blue asbestos from Wittenoom that came down in dirty old ships. The holds weren't ventilated, and conditions were just appalling. The hessian bags the men had to unload were in very poor condition, and some of them had been so badly torn that they burst open when they were handled. Men working in the hatches couldn't see daylight because of all the dust, and their only protection was a piece of cheese cloth over their face. They had massive exposure to asbestos dust. At times they worked ankle-deep in it. Back then, of course, they didn't realise that the cargo they were handling was deadly. They had no idea. I think we can safely assume that many of those men have died because of their exposure to asbestos and that they never knew what killed them. We'll never understand the full extent of the asbestos tragedy on the Fremantle wharves, because we don't know how many wharfies have died of asbestos diseases without being diagnosed.'

Even after port workers became aware that asbestos was dangerous, Rosalie says, there was resistance to health screens. In 1984, an agreement was established for Fremantle waterfront workers to receive ex-gratia payments, generally about $20,000, for asbestos-induced health damage. The big stevedoring companies, such as P&O, Patrick, and the American asbestos company, Manville (formerly Johns Manville), funded the scheme, but initially waterfront workers were wary of having x-rays taken in case they discovered that they had mesothelioma. Undergoing medical tests and having to admit that they had an illness was not something the workers wanted to do, according to Rosalie. It took them a while to warm to the scheme. The amount of compensation paid to workers or their surviving dependants increased over the years, and by the time the scheme ended in 1999, payments were over $50,000.

Rosalie says that one of the problems in administering the ex-gratia payments was the involvement of different trade unions.

'Back then,' she says, 'when the agreement for compensation payments was put in place, there was a union for the waterside workers, one for the shipping clerks and another one for the foremen. Dealing with three unions complicated the situation, but in 1991, they amalgamated into the Maritime Union of Australia. A couple of years later, all the little unions that had amalgamated into the Seamen's Union were also absorbed into the Maritime Union of Australia.

'To get a payment, the wharfies had to go for scans and different tests. If they were knocked back, they could keep trying. It wasn't a problem. I sent them off to the radiology clinic annexed to Royal Perth Hospital and, if they were really sick, I sent them to see Dr Musk at Charlie Gairdner Hospital. Some of our members reported that they'd been told not to return to the radiology clinic because they were fine.

"No," I told them, "you keep going back."

'It wasn't satisfactory, so we got together with the Asbestos Diseases Society. That's when I learned that the scans our members had been having weren't reliable. So we started advising them to go to the Asbestos Diseases Society, and that really fast-tracked the whole process. Scans were done at the Mercy Hospital, which was very good, and Dr Deleuil at the Asbestos Diseases Society referred the men who needed to see a specialist to Charlie Gairdner. We're so fortunate in Western Australia with the specialists we have, like Bill Musk and Bruce Robinson. It's so important.'

In 1999, a landmark High Court ruling opened the way for asbestos-injured waterfront workers to claim common law damages, rendering the ex-gratia payment scheme redundant.

Brian Crimmins, a retired waterfront worker suffering from mesothelioma, had sued the federal government's Stevedoring Industry Finance Committee for damages and won his case in the Supreme Court of Victoria in 1997. An appeal was lodged, but Crimmins died before his case reached the High Court. The High Court upheld the ruling of the Supreme Court of Victoria awarding Crimmins damages of more than $800,000.

The Crimmins case was the first time a waterfront worker sued successfully for an asbestos disease, and it marked a turning point in the battle of waterfront workers to obtain compensation for asbestos-induced injuries.

'The Crimmins case gave wharfies a boost,' says Rosalie. 'They'd been battling to get proper compensation for years, but it had been very difficult to prove which particular stevedoring company or which particular exposure had caused an asbestos disease. The Crimmins case cleared the way, because the High Court ruled that wharfies could sue the federal government's Stevedoring Industry Finance Committee. They now had a defendant they could sue, when previously they'd had none. It was a significant step forward.

'We've co-operated very closely with the Asbestos Diseases Society and the law firm they work with, Slater & Gordon. Without the support the society has given us, it would've been much more difficult to mount cases for compensation. Their president, Robert Vojakovic, told me, "We have to fight every single case." From what I've seen, I'd agree with him. I've seen men still fighting for their compensation payout when they had one foot in the grave.'

Kevin Saint acquired the name 'Pud' when he was a chubby boy at primary school in the late 1930s. As a young man, Kevin followed in the footsteps of his father and got a job on the waterfront at the port of Fremantle. He worked there for thirty-five years, and for most of that time he regularly loaded and unloaded shipments of asbestos. As a result, he suffers from asbestosis.

Kevin's wife remembers him as a bear of a man when he worked on the wharves.

'Pud was huge,' Unis says, 'and it was all muscle. Now look at him – he's as thin as can be.'

Kevin does not look like someone with a serious illness, not in the least. Towering above Unis, he still has the physical presence of a man of great strength, and his thinness does not detract from this impression.

The asbestos tragedy that Kevin has seen in the waterfront community saddens him, but his sense of humour has saved him from becoming morbid. Kevin is the kind of person who moves the air wherever he is, gathering people around him, holding them spellbound with his storytelling and making them laugh.

'There were four children in my family, and I was the youngest. We were typical battlers and lived in a variety of places in the Fremantle area. My father worked on the waterfront, but he was a bit of a gambler unfortunately. At school I did two classes in one year and was dying to turn fourteen so that I could leave. I started at the Fremantle Technical School, where you could learn trades and technical skills in those days, but my mother kept sending me off to apply for jobs. She couldn't get me out to work fast enough, but I was reluctant. Just before Christmas, she arranged an apprenticeship for me through a family friend. I left technical school and started working as an apprentice mattress maker in a furniture factory.'

Unis says, 'I was introduced to Kevin as "Pud". That's what everyone called him. When I was a teenager, I used to watch the South Fremantle Football Club play and go along to their dances on Friday nights. I liked footballers, so did all the other girls. I met Pud one Friday night at the club when I was sixteen and he was eighteen. Three years later we got married. We have one child, our daughter, Rhonda.'

Kevin had a variety of jobs before he started working at Fremantle port in 1956. He remembers the waterfront as a friendly place to work where he had a lot of fun. His workmates were a happy-go-lucky bunch, and there was a lot of humour. He strenuously points out that the popular view of waterfront workers as inherently lazy is a myth. Loading and unloading ships was very hard work, he says, and the bags he carried on his back were heavy. Bags of flour weighed 150 pounds (70 kilograms), and bags of wheat as much as 180 pounds (80 kilograms), and it took a long time for mechanisation to take over from manual labour.

According to Kevin, the corrupt practices that were so prevalent at other Australian ports did not take hold at Fremantle.

'We had very few rorts, and the undesirables we did get from time to time came from other ports like Melbourne or Sydney, where work practices were very different. We called them 'the wise men from the east', because they were real artful dodgers. On the waterfronts in Melbourne and Sydney, there was a lot of dodgy activity, but in Freo it was fairly clear cut. The union had a vigilance officer who toured the wharf to make sure everything was going okay. If there was a problem, it was his job to liaise with the stevedoring company.'

Kevin clearly recalls unloading asbestos cargo. The hessian bags the asbestos arrived in weren't strong enough, and some of them were in such bad condition that they split open when he picked them up. The workers were issued with hooks to lift the bags, but the prongs tore more holes in the hessian. There was nothing scientific about the unloading system, says Kevin. It was very crude.

Once unloaded, the asbestos cargo was stored in sheds on the wharf. The sheds, Kevin recalls, were 'incredibly dusty'. Whenever he handled asbestos, whether in a hatch, on the quayside or in the sheds, the air was thick with dust. When trucks came to take away the asbestos, the dust blew all over the place, especially when it was windy.

In the later years of handling asbestos, shipments of white asbestos from the Manville mines in Canada arrived in better packaging, in bags of plastic, Kevin remembers.

'The American billionaire who ran Manville seemed to get married just about every year,' says Kevin. 'We called him Marrying Tommy, and I reckon he must have had about forty-eight wives.'

In 1991, just after returning from a holiday, Kevin was told by his foreman that the port authority was looking for men to retire voluntarily, because it wanted to reduce its permanent workforce and bring in casual labour. Kevin pulls a face when he remembers the confusion that marked the end of his time on the waterfront. His last day was a Sunday, he says, and the men he was working with were all in a state of uncertainty about what they should do. Should they turn up for work the next day or not? No one seemed to know, not even the men in the office. The men on Kevin's shift believed that this was supposed to be their last day, but they received no official notification.

'Most of us were supposed to finish that day,' says Kevin, 'and a lot of foremen were tied up in that deal. Because we were expecting it to be our last day, we'd organised cartons of beer, but by the evening we still hadn't heard anything officially.

'Men kept asking me if I was finishing, and I had to tell them that I didn't know. It was a shabby way to treat us. All of us more or less decided that we wouldn't turn up for the next shift on Monday.'

'Well,' says Unis, 'I remember that you rang up on Monday, and it sort of became official then, that they didn't want you any more.'

'Yes, that's right. I remember that we were told just to ring on Monday to find out if we still had a job or not. We operated three shifts around the clock – morning, afternoon, and night. They used to put sheets up on the board with the men for each shift the next day. Even if there wasn't much work, all the workers on that shift had to phone in. You had to go to a pick-up point so that you could get "appearance money" when the work was allocated.

'A few weeks after I finished, in December, they organised a special Christmas party for us in the passenger terminal. I thought it was a bit of a guilt trip, because of the way they'd got rid of us. I'm not sure how the stevedoring companies sorted out the redundancy payouts among themselves, but I got $180,000. We lived on that for about three years.'

Four years into retirement, Kevin was diagnosed with asbestosis.

'I honestly was shocked when Pud got the news,' says Unis. 'He always covered his face when he was working with all that dust. He used a cheese cloth. I can remember that, because I used to keep the old ones for cleaning the house.'

'I'd suspected that something was wrong,' Kevin says. 'I could feel a niggle in my back, but I was reluctant to do anything about it because we were about to go on a three-month trip overseas.'

Kevin and Unis both remember receiving the report on the x-rays.

'I nearly died when I read it,' Kevin says. 'It said, "Has this man ever been exposed to, or worked with, asbestos?" I'd had the x-rays done privately, so I went straight to my family doctor. "Yes, there's definitely something there," he told me, "but go on your trip and enjoy yourself. We'll look into this when you get back."'

'When the letter arrived,' Unis says, 'Kevin went over to the window to read it. A good friend was with us at the time, and he whispered to me, "Pud's got asbestosis." It was such a shock, an awful thing. You should've seen Pud on the trip. He was feeling so bad, I nearly got on a plane to take him home.'

The diagnosis of asbestosis was confirmed in January 1996, although Kevin remembers that this involved 'an awful lot of to-ing and fro-ing'. Discovering that he had lost about 30 per cent of his lung capacity worried Kevin, because he had seen a number of his workmates die of asbestos disease. On one day alone, he had three funerals to attend.

Kevin had made a point of visiting men who were sick. On some of these visits he had seen for himself the suffering inflicted by asbestos disease, mesothelioma, in particular. What he noticed about mesothelioma was that people who got it often had another cancer, such as bone cancer, to begin with. Then, all of a sudden, mesothelioma struck them down.

Kevin made an appointment to see the doctor at the Asbestos Diseases Society, Dr Greg Deleuil, who confirmed the diagnosis of asbestosis.

'Greg was a bit annoyed with me, because he thought I wasn't taking it seriously. "I don't know why you're laughing," he said. "You've got a deadly disease." After I saw him, I received $39,000 compensation from the government, but that didn't go far.'

Kevin set about claiming compensation from the Stevedoring Fund, with the help of Robert Vojakovic at the Asbestos Diseases Society.

'You should have seen Robert's old office in North Perth,' he says. 'All these people suffering from asbestos diseases were coming out of the woodwork, and piles of files were stacked high on the floor. You needed a medal for working there.'

Vojakovic referred Kevin to Dr Bill Musk at the Sir Charles Gairdner Hospital. Dr Musk started Kevin on the Vitamin A programme, and Kevin believes that the supplements have made a difference. His health was reviewed once a year by Dr Musk as part of his continuing treatment, but, at his last check-up, Kevin was told to return in two years. He interpreted this as a good sign, and is thankful that he can still mow the lawns and play golf now and then.

Kevin believes that he very nearly missed out on a payout from the Stevedoring Fund. The fund had set a deadline for asbestos-related claims, and he suspects that the fund managers did this, because they knew that there wasn't enough money in the fund to meet the claims they were anticipating.

'I put in a claim before the deadline,' he says, 'and just after I got my payout, the fund went broke. One of the greatest weapons the companies and their insurers have is stringing it out. They're very good at that. It's also important to remember that when you get a payout, there's a list a mile long of costs to pay. You have to pay for scans and x-rays and other medical bills. All those costs are well documented in the health system, and they're all deducted from your payout before you get it.'

Vojakovic helped Kevin obtain another small payout from the stevedoring industry through the law firm Slater & Gordon. Kevin clearly remembers the meeting he attended to negotiate his claim.

'Unis came along with me to an office in the city,' he says. 'I suppose it must have been a law firm. "Sit down in here," they said to us. We were in a kind of alcove, and people kept peeping round the corner at us. I'm not joking. They wouldn't show themselves, because they wanted to see what kind of people they were dealing with. Then they took us into a room. They offered me $25,000. My lawyer said that if I knocked it back, I might not get another offer. He strongly advised me to accept it, so I did. When I received the payout, it was less than I'd expected because of all the costs that had been deducted. I was disappointed about that.

Asbestos became a big health issue among waterfront workers, says Kevin. Anyone who'd worked at Fremantle port had to have x-rays taken, but some of the men who'd worked on the wharves for years never developed an asbestos-related illness.

Kevin regularly comes across former workmates who are sick. He's seen so many men die of mesothelioma, he says, that when he sees a man who's 'not travelling well', he can tell just by looking at him whether or not he's got mesothelioma.

'I hope I never get meso,' he says. 'It's a degrading way to die, because the doctors keep you going so long. They really overdo it. I'd never wish it on anyone.'

Unis says, 'You used to visit quite a few when they were sick, didn't you, Pud? Now they've all gone. You know, when they first started offering x-rays to wharfies in the seventies, I told Pud he should go along, but you didn't want to, did you?'

'What you don't know can't hurt you. I suspect that a lot of the men who've passed away had no idea they were dying because of asbestos, but it's important to remember that other men who worked on the water-front for years don't have a trace of asbestos in their lungs. But at least we all know about it now and, thanks to the Asbestos Diseases Society, we can get x-rays. They organise all that.'

Kevin used to go on weekend golfing trips with friends every now and then. In the late 1990s, his friend Charlie Tyson was sitting behind him in the bus on one of these outings. Charlie was an excellent golfer, Kevin recalls. In fact, Charlie excelled at every sport he tried. On the way home, Charlie tapped Kevin on the shoulder.

'"Pud," he said, "have you ever had anything to do with the Asbestos Diseases Society?"

'"Why do you want to know?"

'"Well, I've got a bit of a problem."'

'"If I were you, I wouldn't hesitate. I've found them an amazing bunch of people. I'm on very good terms with them."'

Thinking about Charlie, Kevin shakes his head. 'He was a real fighter, a very determined man. He insisted on driving when he was very sick, and one day he had a collision. The last time I visited him in hospital, he was just a skeleton with wires coming out of him. It was pathetic.'

May Tyson was married to Charlie for more than fifty years. When Charlie lay dying in hospital, what shocked May, her five children, and everyone else who knew him was that a man of such exceptional strength and will-power could be reduced to such skin and bone.

'It took him six months to die,' May says with tears in her eyes. 'For a healthy man who was always so fit, it was dreadful to see him waste away. Mesothelioma brought Charlie down to nothing.'

May does not often talk about Charlie, because it causes her too much pain to dwell on his illness and the traumatic effect it had on her and her children. Charlie, it is clear, was a man with a personality to match his physical prowess – demanding of himself and everyone around him, and at times intimidating. May is his opposite – gentle, acquiescent, sensitive. Her life revolved around Charlie, so losing him left her feeling adrift. Ever so slowly, however, May is getting used to the idea that she can enjoy herself without Charlie and that living alone need not be lonely.

It distresses May that so little attention has been paid to the asbestos dangers waterside workers were exposed to.

'I don't think the wharfies were ever told that asbestos was so dangerous,' she says, 'so when they started getting asbestos diseases, they didn't know much about them.

When it all came out about Charlie, people just said, "Oh, he's only a wharfie." I'd heard about asbestos diseases, of course, but I never thought that Charlie would be affected. It wasn't something I thought about at all.

'Now wharfies are dying all the time because of asbestos, but I don't think people realise how many of them are affected. You know, there's been a lot in the papers about the miners in Wittenoom, and people getting sick because of asbestos in their homes or whatever, but you hardly ever see anything about wharfies dying because of all the asbestos there was on the waterfront. I don't know why, but you don't.'

One of the hardest aspects of mesothelioma, May thinks, is that there's nothing that doctors can do about it. They can't remove the asbestos fibres from the lung, so that's that. Charlie's case was very severe, she says, so he experienced a lot of pain. His suffering was very hard for him to take, and for her, especially as he'd taken such pride in his physical fitness. Charlie was a natural sportsman who'd played for the South Fremantle Football Club for years and won quite a few trophies, May says. He'd been dedicated to the game, and May believes that he was happiest when he played football for his beloved club. She enjoyed watching him play, and so did her children. They were all very proud of his success on the football field.

Charlie was also a very good cricketer. He was so competitive that he excelled at everything he did, May says. In a way, this made it more difficult for him to cope with mesothelioma. He fought so hard against his illness that people didn't realise how much he was suffering.

'I can remember that Chas started feeling that something wasn't right about two or three years before he was diagnosed with meso,' May says. 'He'd been going along for his usual x-rays, but they never showed anything. When he started feeling worse, he really noticed it because he was such an active man. He went along to talk to his family doctor about it, but nothing came of that either. Eventually, he decided to go along to the Asbestos Diseases Society. I think he might have talked to his friend Kevin Saint about it, but I'm not sure.

'Robert Vojakovic arranged for Chas to have x-rays done at the Mercy Hospital, and I can remember that it was a Saturday afternoon when we found out the result. We were invited to a birthday party that evening, and I can remember Charlie coming home shortly before we were due to leave.

'"Well," he said, "I've got what I always thought I had. It's asbestos. They've given me six months."

'"That's it," I said, "we're not going out tonight, we're staying in."

'But Charlie wasn't having a bar of it. "No, we're not," he said, "we're going to that party."

'We did go to the party, and Charlie enjoyed himself. After that, of course, he started going downhill. He went along to the Asbestos Diseases Society a number of times, and they were very good to him. He used to go to their meetings, because he wanted to find out all he could. He was determined that he wasn't going to let it get him down, but in the end there was nothing he could do. At one point he went into hospital to have a pleurodesis. He knew it wasn't a cure, but he hoped that it would ease the pain. The Silver Chain hospice people were wonderful. They brought him a special bed and a chair, but he couldn't sit up much.'

There was a lot of coming and going at her house, May remembers, during Charlie's last months. Her children came to visit their father, of course, so did friends like Kevin Saint. Kevin was very good, she says, making the effort to come a couple of times a week for an hour or two to keep Charlie company. A doctor popped in now and then, and nurses from Silver Chain came by regularly. As Charlie's disease progressed, he lost a great deal of weight and his muscular arms shrank to little sticks. In the end, all Charlie could do was lie inert in his bed. It was a terrible thing to see.

One day, a church minister came to visit. He told May that Silver Chain had sent him and suggested that it would be a good idea for her to take a break. There was a hospice nearby at the St John of God Hospital in Murdoch, he explained, where Charlie could be taken care of for a few weeks. It was a private hospice, but there would be no cost. May answered that it was Charlie's decision, not hers.

Charlie did not hesitate to say yes. When he left in an ambulance, May sensed that he knew he'd never come home again. Three weeks later, Charlie died.

May did not have a driver's licence, so Silver Chain arranged for her to be driven to the hospice every day and taken home again. It was a comfort to May to see how well Charlie was looked after at the hospice, and she realised that she could not possibly provide the same standard of care at home. Even though the minister had told her that she wouldn't have to pay anything, it surprised May that no one at the hospice ever asked her for money. After Charlie died, she made a donation to show her gratitude.

Charlie's final weeks were a gruelling time for May, but she was not alone in her grief.

'The children weren't too good,' she says, 'because they idolised their father. They'd always been used to him being the strong healthy man that he was. I'm not saying that Charlie was perfect – he could be very hard in some ways – but the children had great respect for him. Our three sons and two daughters are all very family-oriented, and I think that's because of the way they were brought up. They really worshipped Charlie, and they took his death very hard.'

Charlie Tyson was fourteen or so when he left Victoria with his mother and sister after his parents divorced. In Perth, Charlie got a job with a tailor, but it wasn't long before his mother moved the family to Toodyay, a town about 80 kilometres inland. Charlie started working on a farm there, an occupation which exempted him from fighting in the war. May's family owned a farm near Toodyay, and May noticed Charlie in town.

'I used to see him in the street. He was always throwing peanuts in the air and catching them in his mouth. My nephew was a friend of his and introduced us. Soon after that, Charlie asked me to go to the local pictures. It was only in a hall, but I remember that's how it started. We got married about a year later, in 1945, just after the war. We were both very young. Chas was just eighteen and I was nineteen.'

May and Charlie had two children in Toodyay and assumed that they would stay there. Charlie liked farming and May had her family nearby, but in the early 1950s football took them to Perth. Charlie caught the eye of a talent spotter who invited him to play for the South Fremantle Football Club.

For the first few months in Perth, May and Charlie and their children lodged with the mother of the football club's secretary. Then the government gave them a house. Later on, they bought a bigger house of their own where May still lives.

The football club helped Charlie find a job installing gas pipes in Fremantle. The club was where May and Charlie socialised and made friends, and May remembers those years as a happy period in their life together.

Charlie's connections through the football club also

enabled him to move to a better job on the Fremantle waterfront. A lot of footballers worked there, and Charlie really enjoyed being a wharfie. All the work was done manually in those days, May says, and Charlie worked down in the hatches a lot. It wasn't until after he became sick that he realised that all those asbestos fibres must have been flying around him in the hatches.

Charlie used to take off his overalls in the garage and give them a good shake before he gave them to May to wash. He did that, May says, not because he thought the dust was dangerous – that didn't even occur to him – but out of consideration for her. The overalls weren't quite so dusty by the time he'd shaken them, so they didn't make such a mess in the house.

On the waterfront, Charlie worked his way up to become foreman, a position he held for a long time. He worked a lot at night, either from six to eleven in the evening, or from midnight to six the next morning. He expected his men to work, says May, not to sit around and do nothing. He made sure they did their jobs, and May suspects that Charlie was probably more respected than liked at work. For Charlie, she says, everything had to be just right. He was a hard task master.

Charlie spent thirty years on the waterfront and retired when he was sixty. By then, May recalls, he no longer played football, but he went golfing and won quite a few trophies at the Royal Fremantle Golf Club.

'I used to think Chas was such a natural sportsman that he would excel at any sport he played,' she says. 'Now I'm not so sure. I think a lot of it was determination. He was seventy-four when he died. If it hadn't been for asbestos, he'd probably have lived a lot longer.'

May believes that the Asbestos Diseases Society was a great help to Charlie in his final months.

'Robert and Rose Marie Vojakovic are very hard

workers. We used to go along to their support meetings for people with meso, because we didn't know much about the disease at all. About that time, other wharfies were beginning to get asbestos diseases, but they didn't know much about them either. Experts came along to speak to us, and the information they gave was very helpful. At least we got some idea of what to expect. I also think it was good for Charlie to see that he wasn't the only person facing this terrible disease. The meetings always had a very good turnout. They were really marvellous.

'Charlie also went to the Asbestos Diseases Society a number of times to talk to lawyers about his compensation. He got his friends to take him there, but he never took me along. There was a disagreement about the payout, and Charlie used to get very angry that it was taking so long. He couldn't understand why his employers wouldn't pay out graciously rather than force him to fight, and he was determined that they wouldn't get away with it. At the last meeting he was so ill that he had to stay lying down on some chairs the whole time. It was impossible for him to sit up. By then, he was in such a lot of pain. I had morphine tablets to give him, and he used to ask for them, but I couldn't overdo it. When the pain got very bad, a nurse from Silver Chain would come to the house to give him an injection of morphine. That's the state he was in when he was fighting for his compensation. Charlie fought very hard, and the payout came through shortly before he died. After I was left alone, it made a big difference to me financially.

'If anyone deserves compo, it's the men who suffer with mesothelioma. The money doesn't benefit them directly, except to pay for their funeral expenses, but I think they should get it anyway. No one deserves to get such a disease just because they worked in a place where there was asbestos. It's not right, and I think they should be compensated for all their pain and suffering. If I think of Charlie, he did everything right. He had the occasional drink on a Saturday night at the football club, but he never went to pubs, and he didn't smoke. He took his football very seriously and always kept himself fit. His life was his family, sport and work. He stuck to what he believed in, which was doing the right thing. He was too good a man to have to put up with all that before he died.'

Four years after Charlie's death, it still pains May that she was not with him at the end. 'I was there all day and half the night, and then my son and granddaughter took over. In the early hours of the morning I got a phone call from the hospital saying that I needed to get over there straightaway. By the time I arrived, Chas had gone.

'I didn't know until after he died that he'd tried to find out how much his funeral would cost. When the funeral director came to the house, he said, "Your husband came to see me." The funeral was held at the Fremantle Cemetery where we'd bought a plot in the Rose Garden. At the service, the chapel was completely full, and people had to stand outside.

'When people heard that Charlie had meso, they couldn't believe it. When he died, they couldn't believe it. It was a shocking experience, and so unexpected.'

12

Terry Buck has the solid build and wry sense of humour of a man who has spent his working life on the wharves. He grew up in the coastal town of Bunbury, about 150 kilometres south of Perth and, in 1965, he got a job at Bunbury port, where his father and uncles worked. A few years later, Terry moved to Fremantle, to work at the port there. He worked his way up to become the Fremantle branch secretary of the Maritime Union of Australia, a position that brought him into contact with many waterfront workers affected by asbestos disease. Terry remained at the port of Fremantle until he retired in 2002.

According to Terry, it took years before waterfront workers realised what asbestos was doing to them. One of the reasons for this, he thinks, is that it took so long for asbestos diseases to develop. By the time men started dying because of their exposure to asbestos, they were often in their sixties or early seventies. Many of them died 'under suspicious circumstances', and it was often said that they had cancer. When they died, their families contacted the union to enquire about death and funeral benefits, and that's how their deaths became known among the waterfront community.

Terry points out that families got in touch with the union to make their claims once the funeral was over, with the result that autopsies were not conducted and waterfront workers didn't realise that asbestos had caused these deaths. Asbestos was a death sentence, says Terry, and there was nothing the workers could do about it.

Another reason for the asbestos tragedy on the waterfront, Terry believes, is that governments and asbestos companies did everything possible to conceal the truth about asbestos from workers because they feared their industrial strength. Once waterfront unions began to agitate about asbestos exposure, a trust fund was set up to make ex-gratia payments to workers who had become sick because of asbestos. The stevedoring companies and the Manville Corporation put funds into the trust, and the federal government agreed to match their funding dollar for dollar. The real reason for setting up the fund, Terry suspects, was to avert the threat of litigation.

Terry is proud that the waterfront industry was the first to have such a trust fund, but he regrets that dependants were not allowed to make claims from the very beginning. In the early days, he says, if a man failed to make a claim before he died, his family missed out. Once the union realised that this was happening, it pushed for the rules to be changed so that widows and dependent children could also make claims.

The existence of the trust, Terry believes, explains why waterfront workers didn't warm to the idea of co-operating with the Asbestos Diseases Society for quite a while. They thought that they should be able to handle the matter themselves, through their union, and they weren't keen on having x-rays taken. To be fair, Terry says, it was awkward for the men, because they had to go to a clinic in Perth to have x-rays taken. Many of them just didn't want to do that.

Another of Terry's regrets is that the union didn't co-operate with the Asbestos Diseases Society sooner. This delay was the result of politics within the union, he says, and proved detrimental to workers on the Fremantle wharves.

'Having been a union official, I can understand why it happened. When you're an official, you're responsible. At the end of the day, you're the one who gets the blame when something goes wrong.

'You've got to remember that, back in the sixties and seventies, there still weren't that many asbestos victims. At the time, there was a belief within the union that we could handle the issue ourselves. It was only in the late 1980s, when the number of victims began to grow, that the union decided to deal with the Asbestos Diseases Society. We should have put our faith in them much earlier, and it's a tragedy that it took so long.'

In the old days, according to Terry, there were no change rooms for workers on the Fremantle waterside.

'Men used to come to work on push bikes, and they'd go home in their work clothes covered in dust. With the strong winds we get here in Fremantle, you can just imagine how much dust blew off them as they cycled home.

'We used to get dirt money for working in the bad hatches where most of the bags of asbestos had split open. To begin with, it was an extra sixpence an hour, but the men wanted more, and eventually I think we got an extra ten pence. Because they made more money there, the men wanted to work in the bad hatches. That's just human nature.'

The men did not wear masks when they were handling asbestos cargo, Terry says. Cheese cloths were available, but there were never enough of them, and they were far too small anyway. Some of the foremen were regarded as 'real mongrels' who didn't want to give the men anything at all if they could help it. They didn't want to hand out the cloths, because they liked to clean their cars with them. Getting hold of a cheese cloth was like pulling teeth. But even if you were lucky enough to have a cloth, they didn't provide any protection in hatches with no ventilation.

In 1970, regulations were introduced at Fremantle port requiring waterfront workers to wear breathing masks while handling asbestos cargo.

'Considering the massive exposure wharfies had to asbestos dust, it was really pathetic that it took so long,' Terry says.

Waterfront workers were exposed to asbestos dust, even when they weren't handling asbestos cargo. The ships that exported cargoes overseas had asbestos insulation around the pipes and boilers, and bits of asbestos fibre flaked off the lagging constantly, creating dust in the holds.

Figures compiled by the Maritime Union of Australia show that, in the 1960s alone, more than 2500 workers were exposed to asbestos on the Fremantle waterfront. One of the reasons they were exposed to so much dust, Terry thinks, was the condition of the bags the asbestos was packed in. They were second-hand hessian sacks, similar to the kind used for corn. They were tattered and torn, very flimsy, and not properly closed, just folded over at the top.

'What's so terrible is that the wharfies weren't educated about the dangers of asbestos, and they used hooks to lift the sacks onto the sling. As the crane hoisted the sling out of the hold, some of the bags burst open. When that happened, dust showered all over the men and spilled everywhere. It made such a mess on the wharves that the men had to use vacuum cleaners to get rid of it.

'It wasn't unusual for wharfies to be working up to their ankles in asbestos. It wasn't just dust, but lumps of it that accumulated on the deck. Some of the men liked wrestling in it, and some of them used asbestos chips as toothpicks. It's important to remember as well that the men ate their meals on the ships, so, quite literally, they were eating asbestos. Is it any wonder that so many of them have come down with asbestos cancer?

'Unfortunately, Australia has a long history of failure to diagnose asbestos diseases. About ten or twelve years after Australian diggers returned from the First World War, some of them began to die. It was said at the time that they were dying because of the gas they'd been exposed to. But it wasn't gas that killed those soldiers, it was the asbestos inside their gas masks. That's the irony − asbestos was used to protect the soldiers, because it was thought to be indestructible.'

Buddy Durand knows exactly how long he worked on the waterfront − thirty-nine years and seven months. In retirement, he has kept his powerful physique and booming voice and travelled the world. Like his friend Terry, he has remained closely involved with the Fremantle water-front community and watched former workmates die of asbestos disease.

The main thing Buddy remembers about working on the wharves is how much he enjoyed it.

'It was the funniest working environment. You could laugh twenty-four hours a day. In the early days, most of the men were returned diggers from the war. It was all casual labour, there were no rosters, and the foremen had a lot of power. We had to turn up every morning and wait for the foremen to select the gangs for all the ships. The hungry mile, we called it, and a lot of those men were battling to exist from day to day. If you weren't selected, you had to wait to sign your name so that you could get paid for showing up. There was a point system to spread the work about a bit. You got points for each shift you worked and extra points for a night shift. If you were on a night shift, for example, other men had their chance to clock up points the next day, and you had to wait. Equalisation, it was called, but the foremen could still hire and fire. Once the roster system was introduced in the late 1950s, the power of the foremen disappeared, and in 1969 we got permanency.'

Buddy remembers how all the exposed pipes under-neath the decks of the ships were insulated with asbestos lagging. Whenever a forklift banged into the side of the ship, it shook the pipes and asbestos dust from the lagging came down like a shower. The deck hands working above the hatch breathed in a lot of dust, because it went right into their faces as it rose out of the hold. Being a deck hand was something the men strived for, because it took about twenty years of working down below in the hatches before they could get a job on the deck.

Buddy believes that some older ships may still be entering Australian ports with asbestos on board. Products like synthetic rubber and wool have replaced asbestos, but on older ships it's possible, he says, that painted canvas conceals asbestos. It is Buddy's view that the owners of ships flying flags of convenience and operating with Third World crews couldn't care less if their vessels contain asbestos or not.

On the subject of compensation for asbestos victims, Buddy makes the point that the number of cases going to court is falling, and that offers of compensation have been more realistic since the Crimmins case. Class actions are the way that waterfront workers are moving forward, he says, but men who are very ill can't wait for the out-come of a class action and have to fight a lone battle. Charlie Tyson was one of those. Buddy remembers him as a brilliant sportsman, a big strong man with huge shoulders.

'Men like Charlie had to fight hard for compensation,' he says, 'but I'm sure that the lawyers at Slater & Gordon got him the best deal they possibly could. It was unbelievable to see the way Charlie was at the end. It shocked everyone.'

Fremantle waterfront workers have been very badly affected by asbestos disease, Buddy says, pointing out that men are dying all the time. Most of them are retirees, and as many as nine have died in a single month. For Buddy, asbestos is a cursed thing.

Allan Shaw, known to everyone as 'Pop', spent twenty-eight years on the Fremantle waterfront. His work on ships – loading and unloading, driving winches and cranes – exposed him to sunlight and its reflection off the water. This exposure caused severe damage to Allan's skin, disfiguring his face.

'I've had that many malignant skin cancers removed that I'm a walking time bomb. I have to see the doctor once a month, and every time he cuts some more out of me. I've had surgery for facial reconstruction, more than two thousand treatments to my face, legs and arms, about fifty malignant cancers removed, half my ear cut off, and a hundred and sixty stitches down my chest – all due to skin cancer.'

Allan joined the waterfront when he was thirty-one.

'I'd worked as a roof tiler for sixteen years before then, but I wanted to get out because it was such hard manual work in those days. Those tiles were heavy – they weighed 9 pounds [4 kilograms] each. When we retiled the roof of St Patrick's Church in Fremantle, four of us carried 99 tons of tiles onto that roof over a seven-month period. It was very, very hard work. That's why I started looking for something else. I applied to be a tally clerk on the wharves, but I didn't get the job. In those days, there was the father-and-son rule – if your father was a wharfie, you were first in. By the time I got on the wharves, they'd dropped that rule and every kind of tradesman worked there – motor mechanics, plumbers, carpenters, bricklayers, cabinet makers, even market gardeners. They went there because they got a lot more money.'

Allan used to look forward to going to work. What he liked most about the waterfront was that every day was different. The kind of cargo he handled changed all the time – timber, crayfish, phosphate, all sorts. There was quite a social life, too, and he enjoyed that. There were social clubs, two football teams, a darts team, and a lot of the men played golf.

Allan clearly remembers going down into the hatches to clear away the asbestos that had spilled.

'I remember that the bags used to break, and the blue asbestos would spill everywhere. It would get in my hair, my eyes, on my face, all over me. When we finished unloading the boats, there was always loose asbestos on the floor that had to be swept up and put into the save-all. I used to shovel it into the save-all, which was a flat piece of canvas with ropes sewn underneath it. When we put the ropes on the hook, the canvas looked like a big bag. It was very dusty work, and when I was sweeping up all that broken asbestos, a big cloud went up. You could hardly see the sun through it. When we were working at night, there were clusters of ten or twelve light bulbs over each corner of the hatch so that we could see what we were doing. They were the kind of lights you see on old tennis courts and bowling greens, and they hung on cords over the sides of the ship. When you were working with asbestos at night, it was the same thing – when you looked up at those lights, you saw this big cloud of dust.'

The bags of asbestos were stacked high, and Allan used a wool hook to get a better grip on them. The hook didn't work very well and often ripped the bags. The bags were put into a rope sling, drawn out of the hold and dropped on the docks. The whole time the bags were being hoisted out of the hold, Allan says, dust hung thick all around him, but he had no idea that it was dangerous to breathe it. Nobody knew. The men were never warned about the dust, so they didn't know that it could give them cancer.

According to Allan, the men didn't take much notice of the asbestos dust because they were used to working in dust from the different kinds of cargo they handled. Dust came off wheat, and timber destined for export, and the superphosphate that farmers imported for use as fertilisers. He remembers that asbestos dust used to make his mouth and nose feel dry, but he didn't pay any attention because sulphur dust was so much worse. The sulphur was used for chlorine for swimming pools, and the dust burned his eyes. Allan didn't have goggles, so he just put milk on his eyes to stop them watering.

'Some of the men messed around a bit with the asbestos,' Allan says. 'I mean, all of us used to sit on the bags and lie on them sometimes, but some of the men rolled bits of asbestos in their fingers to make a moustache, and some of them chewed on it like chewing tobacco. The only protection we had was cheese cloths, and we got them because of all the wheat dust. When I handled asbestos, I had to keep shaking my cloth all the time because it got so clogged up with dust.

'Some real old rubbish ships used to come into Fremantle, and working with blue asbestos was always a dirty dusty job. The blue asbestos from Wittenoom stopped coming in the late 1960s, but I can't remember exactly when. I also unloaded a lot of the white asbestos that came from Canada or the United States. It used to come in different bags. I remember they were square block bags. They were compressed, and dust wasn't so much of a problem.'

Conditions on the wharves were very primitive when Allan first started working at Fremantle port. When he was down in the freezer holds, where crayfish were loaded for export to the United States, he felt as if his nose and ears would snap off because they were so cold. He was lucky, though. Special boots were introduced for work in the freezer holds, just before he got a job at the port. Before then, men wrapped hessian around their boots as protection against the freezing temperatures. There was always the fear, Allan says, that the crayfish might start to thaw, so the temperatures in the freezer holds were kept very low.

Allan says that workers at the port were identified by numbers, not by their names.

'At the weekend the roster went up with all the numbers. When you rang the office, you always gave your number. When I started, there were about 1800 men on the wharf, and my number was 1634. By the time I left, the numbers were down, and I was number 594.'

Allan was a keen sportsman and kept himself very fit. He won a state yachting championship in 1952, when he was seventeen or so, and two years later he started as a trainer at the Claremont Football Club in Perth. In 1962, he became the club's head trainer. At the time, he was the youngest head trainer of any football club in the country, and he stayed on in the role until 1985. At the Swan Yacht Club, Allan worked his way up to become commodore, and was made a life member of the club in 1996. He still does voluntary work there, but he can't jump from boat to boat any more. Hey, Pop, people used to say to him, you jump just like a monkey.

But those days are over, and now Allan can't do much of anything.

Allan retired in 1993, but continued working on the waterfront for another year.

'I was on the B Reserve. It's like a reserve pool of wharfies. The foremen used to love the old blokes going back because we knew everything.'

Ten years or so after he retired, Allan began to notice pain in his back and chest. He felt a little breathless now and then, but the first time he had to stop to catch his breath was a shock.

'The first time I realised I was running out of puff was when I went to Tommy Bottrell's funeral. I knew Tommy very well. He was a wharfie and the head trainer at the South Fremantle Football Club for many years. In his youth, Tommy was a state sprinter, and he was always a very fit man. He was very popular, and, when he died of mesothelioma, everyone went to his funeral. Afterwards, everyone was supposed to get together at the South Fremantle Football Club for drinks, so I walked back to my car to drive over there. And that's when it happened. I got so puffed out I had to stop. I couldn't work out what was wrong with me, because I thought I was travelling really well. I'd seen a lot of wharfies going off, and I kept saying, Jeez, how lucky am I?

'I was getting tireder all the time. I was running out of breath, and I had a dry cough. I kept saying to myself, If only I could take a deep breath and open up my lungs! My family doctor sent me off for an x-ray. It showed a bit of a cloud on my lung, but the doctor at the hospital said I'd be all right. My family doctor pre-scribed Vitamin C tablets and told me to drink plenty of water and see him again in a month. The pain got worse, I still had the cough, and I got very bloated. I used to have a couple of beers, so I thought I was blown up because of the beer. But it turned out to be the fluid that was making me so puffed up. I couldn't even bend over to tie my shoelaces.'

The next x-ray showed that part of Allan's lung had collapsed. There was also fluid on the lung, so Allan was sent to Fremantle Hospital to have the fluid removed and tested.

Allan remembers the doctor asking him, 'Are we hurting you?'

'"No," he said, "I'm just bored", but, as the fluid drained, he felt as if his lung was being pulled up and up. He could see the fluid coming out of him, trickling out of a tube into a clear glass container. It was dark and looked like urine. He thought it might have been lying around his lung for quite a while. When he was told the results of the tests, Allan learned that mesothelioma cells had been detected.

Fluid quickly accumulated on his lung again, so Allan went back into hospital. Every day, a nurse took a sample of blood from him. When he saw her coming, Allan said, 'Oh, here comes the vampire!' He remembers that two tubes were inserted into his back and that four pieces of tissue were taken out of him for testing. The results of the biopsy confirmed that he had mesothelioma.

'So, there it was. All that time I thought I was travelling so well, then *bang* I had it.'

Reflecting on the toll asbestos disease has taken on waterfront workers, Allan says, 'So many have died. The last time I saw the lawyer, I asked him, "How many whar-fies have got claims in for asbestos?" "I can't tell you that," he said.'

Money, Allan says, means nothing to him. He's not worried about it at all. He has, however, made sure that his wife and three sons have been well provided for. His sons are doing just fine – two are in the merchant navy and one is working in a restaurant in Queensland. They've all got their own houses, and they know that their father is coming to the end of the road. Allan's lawyer is working on his compensation claim. He assures him that he won't have to pay fees if his claim is not successful. Allan's family and friends keep telling him to go away and enjoy himself, but he doesn't feel like it.

'I've copped this,' he says, 'but I don't like people bogging me down – talking for the sake of talking. Once word got around that I had meso, I got hundreds of phone calls from people who'd known me for years. Now I don't answer the phone, because I don't like people going on and on about grandma's remedies. When I meet people, it's always the same thing, You're looking well, they say, there's nothing wrong with you, you'll be all right … you know, asbestos got a mate of mine, and he lived for ten years and did this and that. They hold me up with a lot of rubbish. My wife answers the phone now, and she's feeling the strain a bit.'

Allan met Kaye at a dance and married her in 1961. He is very proud of her, pointing out that she was one of the first women to qualify for the swimming race to Rottnest Island in 1958, one of the first all-female crew of the Fremantle Sailing Club, and a top division lawn bowler. Life with Kaye, Allan says, has been really interesting and varied and, since he retired, they've travelled overseas together, as they'd always planned to do.

Since retiring Allan has also spent a lot of time with his friend Ken McGuire, whom he has known for twenty years. They sailed from Darwin to Fremantle together, and Allan sometimes went bush with Ken when he was surveying for mining tenements. In the bush they walked 15 kilometres a day cutting back scrub and trees along the way. Allan is very glad that he had those experiences, because now he can't even do the gardening and handyman jobs at home.

George O'Cass spent much of his working life at naval dockyards – on Garden Island in Sydney Harbour, and on the other Garden Island in Australia, just a few kilometres offshore from Perth. He is now an officer of the Dust Diseases Board of New South Wales and sees firsthand the tragedies that asbestos has caused.

'In the fifties and sixties, asbestos was the wonder product that was used for everything. People had no idea that it could kill them. They just didn't know. Later on, when it began to be reported in the news that asbestos was dangerous, people just thought they had to be careful around it. For example, some men drank a pint of milk to line their stomach so as "not to swallow anything". Drinking milk didn't make a blind bit of difference, of course, and that's one of the things that's so sad.

'The men who were working on those naval ships were breathing in asbestos dust all the time. It was inevitable. Asbestos was used as a flame retardant right throughout naval vessels. In the gun turrets, for example, there was raw asbestos inside the walls. It was considered wonderful stuff because it heated up and cooled down, but it didn't burn. The men who constructed and refitted ships and submarines and the sailors who went out to sea on them were exposed to massive amounts of asbestos dust. The dust was all-pervasive in those enclosed spaces, so it's little wonder so many of those men have died because of asbestos.

'For twenty years or more, the men on the dockyards didn't know what asbestos could do to them, because they were never told. Thousands were involved. Once word did get out about the danger, if anyone dared to say anything, the answer they got was, Shut up, otherwise you won't have a job. I wouldn't be surprised if the result of all that dishonesty and intimidation will be the next big body of asbestos claims.'

Ross Gardener also worked at naval dockyards for many years and sits on the Dust Diseases Board of New South Wales.

'I don't think management of the dockyards thought there was anything wrong with asbestos until the 1980s,' Ross says. 'The navy told them that it was okay. I don't think people realised what the long-term effects of asbestos were going to be. Those who knew didn't care.'

Merv Whitehouse spent nineteen years repairing and refitting naval vessels on Garden Island and Cockatoo Island in Sydney. As a result, he has asbestosis and has lost 30 per cent of his lung capacity.

According to Merv, fire prevention was the top priority on naval ships. Anything to do with heat and flame had a thick asbestos cover around it, he says, because asbestos was considered an essential fire retardant. Boilers were encased in asbestos lagging 6 inches thick, with only the valves exposed for turning on and off, and all the pipes were wrapped in asbestos as well. Machinery and equipment of all kinds had asbestos in them, including the cookers in the kitchens.

Welders used an asbestos cloth to protect their faces against sparks, and they blew away asbestos dust with a high-pressure air hose before they started welding. They had to remove the dust to prevent imperfections in their welds, but blasting it away exacerbated the dust problem in the enclosed spaces where they worked.

Concerns about asbestos didn't start to come to a head until the late 1970s, Merv recalls, and that's when welders started vacuuming the dust or spraying it with water.

'Asbestos was used everywhere on naval vessels, and it flaked off the lagging all the time. Blue asbestos was used extensively on aircraft carriers like the *Vengeance*, *Sydney*, and *Melbourne*. Even worse was *The Duchess*, the frigate the Brits offloaded onto the Australian navy. It was full of asbestos, a real mess. The older the ships were, the worse their condition.'

Merv remembers that there was constant dust on all the ships, but more on some than others.

'The aircraft carriers were definitely the worst. They were completely encased in asbestos. When planes landed on the flight deck, the asbestos came down like snow underneath the deck.

'Destroyers were also bad. When guns were fired, the ship would shake, and bits of asbestos would come down all over the place.

'When we were refitting a ship, dismantling the lagging created one big mess.

'Stripping asbestos from turbines and boilers was a grim job. The lagging was taken away in truckloads, and the dust was so bad I could have been in the mill at Wittenoom. I swept it away, but no sooner did the deck look brand-new, than there was the same amount of dust again. I used to ask myself, Where's it all coming from?'

Computers in the consoles had to be covered before repair work started, Merv recalls, so that dust did not get into them. The irony was that dust got into the computers anyway, because the cloths covering them were made of asbestos. Merv believes that the navy people in charge were more concerned about asbestos dust getting into their computers than into the men's lungs. He also thinks that they must have known about the danger, saying that American insurance companies hadn't insured people working with asbestos since the 1930s. He never heard a word from the navy about any possible danger associated with asbestos, and he feels certain that this was a deliberate ploy to keep workers ignorant about the danger they were exposed to. What the senior navy personnel were doing, he says, was plain murder.

Merv believes that there are significant differences in the way employers deal with asbestos claims.

'The department of navy seems to be coming to the party, all right,' he says. 'If you go through the proper channels, you can get compensation without too much hassle. I've talked to so many people about this, and I think most of them didn't have too many problems getting compensation unless they were dealing with James Hardie. That company is brutal. Once you sue them, you're on the merry-go-round. They keep you at arm's length just waiting until you die. That's how they are. Then there's the other extreme. One of the blokes I knew through the bowling club told me one day that he had meso. He must have got it in England, because that's where he worked. Anyway, he got straight on the phone, and five or six months later he got a payout. He got quite a considerable amount.'

Merv participates in the Vitamin A programme run by the Sir Charles Gairdner Hospital in Perth.

'It's still called a trial, and every year I receive a letter with a questionnaire from Charlie Gairdner. My family doctor makes the arrangements for me to have blood tests and x-rays and then sends the results back to Perth. If they're happy with the results, they send me a year's supply of the Vitamin A supplements. Even though I'm on the other side of the country, the programme works very well. I really think the supplements have helped stabilise my lung condition, so I just keep going.'

PART 5

AN ORDINARY JOB

13

The resistance of asbestos to corrosion and friction made it an essential component in vehicle brake linings and clutch pads. In the course of their daily work, thousands of motor mechanics disturbed dust from these asbestos materials during the cleaning, servicing and replacement of brakes and clutches. In doing so, they unknowingly risked their lives.

Legislation introduced in Australia on 1 January 2004 prohibited the use of asbestos materials in the production and servicing of transport vehicles, but it did not require pre-existing asbestos materials to be removed from vehicles produced before that date. This legislative shortfall left motor mechanics around Australia at continued risk of asbestos exposure.

Tony Lopresti was a motor mechanic for thirty-five years. He was happiest when he had a car to tinker with, and it was accepted among his family and friends that he lived for his work.

A small, agitated man, Tony paces about punching his hands in the air and gasping for breath. He cannot be still. Having been active all his life, he tries to fight the inactivity that he has been condemned to, and this struggle compounds his distress. Tony is one of the asbestos casualties of the automotive repair industry, a man driven to despair by his illness and the unfairness of what has happened to him.

Tony grew up in Sicily and emigrated to Australia when he was twenty-one. He arrived in Perth in February 1970 and found a job as a motor mechanic within a few weeks.

'In those days, the Ford Motor Company had a big service centre right in the city on Adelaide Terrace. I told the boss at Centre Ford that I'd been to technical school in Italy for a while and worked on push bikes and motor bikes. "I've got a few Italians working here," he said, "and they're all very good workers. They never cause any problems. You've been straight with me, so I'll give you a chance." A couple of weeks later, he told me I was good enough and gave me a job.'

In 1972, Tony received a promotion at work and got married. His wife, Connie, came from a family of Italian immigrants and had grown up on a farm at Southern Cross, about 120 kilometres east of Perth. At Centre Ford, Tony was delighted to be selected for the Quick Service area. Five of the company's best mechanics worked there, servicing thirty to forty vehicles a day. They earned more than their colleagues in the main workshop, but they also had to work fast and do a lot of overtime hours.

Quick Service, Tony explains, was a very small space with two pits for servicing four cars at a time. Working underneath the cars was the dirtiest job, and the men took it in turns to work in the pits. Tony remembers that the brake linings had asbestos fibre in them, and that the fibre created a lot of dust. The dust had to be removed before brakes could be serviced, so he blew it away with a high-pressure air hose. All the mechanics did this, and at times the dust was almost unbearable. Tony never complained, because he accepted that mechanics had to put up with dusty conditions. The thought that the dust might be dangerous did not occur to him.

'I was at Centre Ford for five years,' says Tony. 'I really liked it there, but I left because Connie's father asked me to help him on the farm. I invested some of my savings to put in wheat and barley crops, but 1975 was a very dry year. We couldn't harvest the crops because of the drought, and I lost my investment. I left the farm after only ten months and went to work at the Ford car dealership in Narembeen.

'The owner, Col Commins, promised that he'd supply me with accommodation, because Narembeen was more than 100 kilometres from the farm, too far for me to drive every day. I lived with him for several months before I could move into a State Housing Commission house and bring my family to live with me. Col kept his word and paid my rent for the thirteen years we lived in that house. Col was a very good employer, and I really liked working for him.'

Tony left Narembeen because he thought that the journey to the nearest high school in Merredin, about 30 kilometres away, was too arduous for his children. At the beginning of the school year in 1988, he sent his wife and three children back to Perth. He followed them several months later, once his employer found a mechanic to replace him.

In Perth, Tony found a job as a motor mechanic at a Gull service station. He stayed there until 1993 when he moved to a garage in Osborne Park, just a few minutes from his home. He got on very well with his new employer, Tom Radis, who gave him generous bonuses and invited him to dinner now and then.

'At Tom's garage, I can remember that I started cleaning brakes with a water hose instead of air. By then, there was talk about asbestos, but I never ever thought it would affect me. Tom's workshops were spotless. I mean, the floor was so clean you could eat off it. I wasn't breathing any dust there but, by 1998, I was starting to feel sick. I tried to ignore it, but I was getting tired. After I ate my sandwich at lunch time, I had to lie down on the couch in the back room and have a rest. Sometimes I fell asleep. I couldn't help it. "Take it easy, Tony," Tom said, "there's no rush. You don't have to work so hard."

'In all the places I've worked, I've never had another boss who told me not to work so hard. After about a year of this, I felt so bad one morning that I went to see my GP. He sent me to see a heart specialist. After that, I had to take medication for bronchitis for a while, but it didn't make me feel any better.'

In early 1999, Tom Radis retired. Tony continued to work at the garage for the new owner, Steve Martino, but his health problems were making his life a misery.

'I wasn't feeling well at all,' he says, 'and my GP kept sending me for x-rays and tests. The doctors always asked me if I'd ever smoked. I told them, no, I'd never smoked in my life. In July 1999, I had an appointment to see Dr Robinson at Charlie Gairdner Hospital. That time I finally found out what was wrong with me. I remember it very clearly, because it was my fiftieth birthday. Dr Robinson said to me, "You can't work any more, Tony, you've got asbestosis." I couldn't believe what I was hearing. I asked him, "How can I have asbestosis when I've never worked with asbestos?"'

Professor Robinson explained to Tony that blowing asbestos dust out of brakes had cost him 40 per cent of his lung capacity. This made Tony very angry. He was aware that asbestos diseases had killed a lot of Wittenoom workers, but he'd never read anything in the papers about motor mechanics getting these diseases or even heard of such a thing. It was inconceivable to him that servicing cars had made him sick.

At the garage, Tony explained to his boss what had happened. Steve Martino was sympathetic and told him to take a month's holiday. When you've had a good break, he said, we'll see if you can come back.

Tony did as he was told, but he was anxious to get back to work. He planned to retire at fifty-five and was loath to lose any of his superannuation benefits. Martino let him return to the garage after a month, but soon realised that he was in no fit state to work. Tony felt very tired all the time, as if he was about to fall asleep, and he had to leave.

Fixing cars was Tony's passion, and he was inconsolable when he had to give it up. With no income, he had to send his wife out to work. Connie got a job at the local supermarket, working extra shifts in the evenings and at weekends to earn more money.

Tony turned to the Asbestos Diseases Society for help. Robert Vojakovic explained to him that he was legally entitled to receive compensation for his illness, and that his various employers had made contributions on his behalf to the workers' compensation scheme run by the state government. Steve Martino's insurer would have to pay, he said, because Steve had been his last employer. That was how the law worked, and it didn't matter that Steve had employed him for only a few months.

Tony sold his boat and started dipping into his savings so that he and Connie could get by financially. He had doctors' fees to pay and drugs to buy but, just when he really needed it, he had to give up his private health insurance policy because he could no longer afford the premiums.

'Everywhere I went,' he says bitterly, 'it cost me money.'

The less he was able to do, the more ill-tempered Tony became. He had to bring in handymen to do jobs in the house and garden he'd always done himself, and he found that he had to keep lying down to catch his breath. It was clear to him that his fractious behaviour was affecting his family, but he couldn't contain his anger. He felt an overwhelming sense of injustice that he had an asbestos disease, even though he'd never worked for an asbestos company, and he railed against his misfortune.

The wrangling over compensation further fuelled Tony's rage. He expected to receive an offer of $130,000, the usual amount paid as a lump sum from the workers' compensation scheme at the time. When he received the first offer on the telephone, he lost his temper. "Do you know what you can do with $30,000?" he yelled. "You can buy a box of matches and burn yourselves." In the end, he went to court.

'It was actually a room in an office building,' he says, 'not a real court. The review officer who heard my case was a very nice lady, and everyone sat around a big long table. Robert was acting for me, and sitting opposite us were the lawyers for the insurance companies that didn't want to pay me any compensation.'

Tony's workers' compensation claim involved his five former employers in the automotive repair industry. Each company had a different insurer, and several of the insurance companies were re-insured. The insurers and re-insurers all retained the services of different law firms.

It took two years to resolve the matter. In October 2002, Tony's case went before the Compensation Magistrate's Court. By this time, the state government's insurer, SGIO, had agreed to pay Centre Ford's share of Tony's compensation entitlement, given that the business no longer existed, and Col Commins was also willing to make his proportional contribution.

The case was heard by a review officer of the state body responsible for enforcing the *Workers' Compensation and Rehabilitation Act 1981*, Workcover Western Australia. Robert Vojakovic represented Tony in his claim for workers' compensation benefits brought against the three remaining employers – the Gull service station, and the garage owned by Tom Radis and later Steve Martino. The insurers of all three businesses claimed that they were not liable.

At the hearing, a government occupational hygiene expert gave evidence relating to the dangers of asbestos dust inhalation in workplaces where cars were serviced. He described spraying water as the best way to remove asbestos dust, but pointed out that a small amount of dust would always be present in such workplaces. Using a high-pressure air hose was the worst method of removing asbestos dust, he said, because it vigorously disturbed the dust, thereby increasing the likelihood that workers would inhale it.

Tony's supervisor at Centre Ford's Quick Service told the court that he was so concerned about the amount of dust in the workshop that he asked management to install a dust extractor. The fan that was installed in the ceiling sucked up a lot of dust, but the asbestos dust that accumulated in the pits, where mechanics worked all the time, remained trapped underneath the cars.

In their evidence, Tom Radis and Steve Martino said that their business premises were kept clean at all times, and that water was sprayed to remove dust. Martino also said that there was medical evidence to prove that Tony had already been ill by the time he employed him.

In his questioning of Tom Radis, Vojakovic wanted to know about a statement he had signed.

'You gave a statement to a private investigator, I'm led to believe. Is this correct?'

'Yes.'

'Did that gentleman tell you who he represented?'

'I wasn't really sure at the time I was with him.'

'If you can have a look at the statement, please, is that your signature at the bottom of the page?'

'I remember the person now. He wrote this actually ... yes, I remember – '

'And that's your signature on it?'

'Yes.'

At the close of the two-day hearing, the review officer cited a number of previous cases relevant to Tony's before handing down her decision that Steve Martino's company was Tony's last employer and therefore liable to pay him compensation.

Tony remembers Martino's reaction to the decision.

'Steve was pretty upset. He thought it was unfair, because I'd only been working for him for such a short time. He was going to try to force the other companies to pay some of the cost, but that won't have been easy. Since he was forced to pay, I've been getting cheques every fortnight, but they're not enough to live on. When they reach the ceiling of $130,000, they'll stop. What will we do then?

'Before I got asbestosis, I never took a sick day off work. I never even thought about it. When my children started working, I said to them, "Even if you're on your death bed, you never take a day off sick." I used to walk a few kilometres around the neighbourhood every morning and that kept me quite fit, but after I got sick it was stop and start, stop and start. I couldn't even get around the block. Now I'm scared of doing any exercise at all, because the doctors warned me that I could get a stroke if my heart has to work too hard. About the only thing I can still do is drive. I take the car to the shops, and sometimes I drive into town to meet my friends at the Italian Club.'

Tony's chief concern is to provide for his family. On the advice of Robert Vojakovic, he got in touch with the law firm Slater & Gordon to make a common law claim for negligence against Steve Martino's company. He was confident that his claim would be successful and that his payout would see his family comfortably set up, but he encountered an unexpected problem: Tom Radis had signed an affidavit saying that he had suffered from cancer of the oesophagus and that he had undergone chemo-therapy treatment for his illness.

Tony was flabbergasted when his lawyer, Tim Hammond, delivered this news.

'I've never had cancer. Ever since I heard about the affidavit, I've been trying to work out why Tommy said such a thing. What makes it so hard to understand is that he was so good to me. The only explanation I can come up with is that the insurance companies offered him a big sum of money so that they could put the whole thing on hold. I think they want to drag the whole thing out as long as possible. Maybe they're hoping that I'll get so sick that I just give up, but if that's what they're thinking they're in for a surprise.'

Tony's lawyer advised him that it would take some time to go through all his medical records provided by doctors in different locations. Tony realised that there was nothing he could do but wait, so he decided to go away for a while.

'In a few days I'm going to Sicily to see my mother. She's 93 years old, and I want to see her while I can. This is my last chance.

'I'll be glad to get away from Perth. When I first came

here, I felt so lucky. I thought that Perth was paradise with so many beautiful beaches and open spaces and sunshine all year. I knew I could have a good life here if I worked hard, so that's what I did.

'I thought being a motor mechanic was just an ordinary job. It never entered my head that it would kill me. The companies that made asbestos brake linings knew that men like me would die if they breathed asbestos dust. They knew that even before I arrived in Australia. They continued to use asbestos for all those years, but no one ever told me that my job was dangerous.

'The irony is that I loved my work, just loved it. It was the one thing I was really good at.'

Tony's wife is continuing to work all the hours she can at the supermarket down the road while Tony is away. Connie suffers from insomnia, brought on, she says, by all the stress. The sofa in the living room is the only place where she can fall sleep, but her respite is always brief, just a few hours in the early morning. At work she hides her exhaustion behind a chirpy manner, and at home she keeps the blinds permanently drawn to conserve her energies in the restfulness of the dark.

'If anyone had told me that Tony would get asbestosis because he was a motor mechanic, I would have laughed at them. Never ever in a million years would I have thought of that. You think of miners and the people who actually make things with asbestos, but a motor mechanic – no, never.'

Connie is well aware that she and her children were exposed to asbestos dust for years, because Tony brought it home with him on his work overalls. The children used to jump all over him, Connie remembers, and his overalls were really filthy. He had four pairs, and there was so much grease and dust on them that they had to be washed separately. Connie assumed that oil and petrol made the overalls so 'clammy', never thinking that it was asbestos dust.

Tony also came into contact with other people when he was wearing his work overalls.

'Tony's work didn't finish when he came home,' Connie says. 'He was always getting phone calls from people asking him to fix their cars. If someone called him on a Sunday and said their car had broken down, Tony would go and fix it. He couldn't leave anyone stranded, that's the way he was.'

Connie thinks that Tony has become a different person in the six years since he left the workforce. He was never able to sit around and do nothing, and that didn't change when he found that he had asbestosis. His physical limitations caused him enormous frustration, his financial worries weighed heavily on him and his life became 'a real hassle'.

'When Tony put in his claim for workers' compo, we thought it would go through pretty quickly because of the medical report. We didn't expect to have to fight every step of the way for what he was legally entitled to, but that's what happened.'

Tony's common law claim is proving to be another battle, and Connie lets out a snort of disgust when she thinks of the trouble Tom Radis has caused.

'The medical records will prove that Tom's statement is a sworn lie. How could Tony have chemo when he never took a sick day off work? You can't go to work if you're having cancer treatment, you just can't do it. Besides, I'm Tony's wife, and I would've known for sure if he was having chemo. The funny thing is that Tom had already left the garage when Tony was diagnosed with asbestosis. He had nothing to do with the business by then, so why would he say such a thing?'

What makes the saga even more baffling for Connie is that she used to regard Radis as 'a fantastic person'. His considerate treatment of Tony at work impressed her, and she appreciated his efforts to engage Tony socially. Connie wanted to telephone Radis to discuss his statement, but Tony wouldn't allow it. Let the lawyers deal with it, he told her.

'This latest setback has made Tony worse,' Connie laments. 'He's tired because he can't get enough oxygen into his body, and he's irritable because of all the stress. On top of everything else, he's somehow got it into his head that everyone is against him. "You all want me dead before my time," he says. "You want me in my grave." I don't think he realises what he's saying, but he's making it very hard on us.

'I'm dreading the day when he can't hop into his car and visit his friends any more. If it gets to the stage when he can't drive and he needs someone to look after him all the time, then I'll have to give up work. That's when we'll have real financial problems.

'The only thing I can be certain of is that Tony isn't going to get any better, because there's no cure for asbestosis. I try not to stress out too much, so that I'll be strong enough for whatever happens. These past few years have been a real eye opener for me. The way some people have behaved has been shocking. It's been an awful time, an absolute nightmare.'

Stephana is the youngest of Tony's children. In her father's absence, she has moved back into the family home to keep her mother company. She feels her father's tragedy keenly, but focuses on providing her mother with the support she needs and developing her own professional and personal life.

'My father's illness has affected him more mentally than

physically, I think. He was a very dynamic person before, never stopped still. Now he just mopes around.

'Before he left for Italy, he was very demanding and irritable. Now I know why. I didn't find out about the statement by Tom Radis until after he left. I was quite shocked, because I thought Tom was a good friend of the family.

'My father really needed a break, so it's good that he's gone to Italy. When he arrived, his relatives were alarmed by his shortness of breath. Not long after he got over there, he spent more than a week in hospital. Now he's on oxygen at least eighteen hours a day.

'The financial situation plays on his mind more than anything else, I think. He very much wants to support the family. That's how he shows his love for us – by making sure we have a roof over our heads and food on the table.

'The affidavit has added a nasty twist to the whole thing. I think the insurance companies have done this so that they can stretch things out and gain time, but it's perjury. There's gaol time associated with that.

'What's happened to my father has changed me. I keep thinking that, if only they'd known then what they know now about asbestos, a lot of lives could have been saved.'

PART 6

GATHERING FORCES

14

In the office on Main Street, Robert and Rose Marie Vojakovic are starting a normal working day of back-to-back meetings.

'You know,' Robert says, 'we've been fighting these asbestos companies for twenty-five years, and we've had some success, but that doesn't mean we can slack off, not one bit. We have to be very thorough in preparing test cases against them. All documents – medical records, testimonials, whatever – must be meticulously assembled. The companies involved couldn't care less. They're very callous, and getting them to pay compensation isn't easy.'

'We've got about ten thousand members now,' says Rose Marie, 'and in the past year Robert has helped five hundred members write their wills, and I've attended two hundred funerals. More and more, I'm working with people suffering from mesothelioma. Recently, people have been going down like nine pins with it. We've been overwhelmed, and so have the doctors.

'One of the ways we help people with meso is to invite them to meetings where oncologists and respiratory and pain specialists, among others, come along and give a talk. Many people who get mesothelioma really have no idea of what's going to happen to them. When they're given the diagnosis, it often comes as a bolt out of the blue, so they're anxious to find out what to expect. At the meetings, they're in a non-threatening environment and can be totally relaxed. They learn all sorts of things that can be very valuable to them, and we always spoil them with a yummy afternoon tea.

'Mesothelioma is extremely painful, and fighting the pain is a battle. One of the things that makes meso such a cruel disease is that it's so difficult to control the pain. It really is torture. What's happening to all these people with asbestos diseases should never have happened. It's a massacre. That's the only way I can describe it.'

In the reception area, people are waiting to see Dr Deleuil. He has just returned from a trip to the United Kingdom where he gave a presentation about Wittenoom called 'Blue Murder Down Under' to asbestos victims' organisations in cities around England, Scotland, Wales and Northern Ireland.

'The last thing I show them on the screen,' he says, 'is a photograph of my mother sitting by a window in our house in Darwin where I grew up. She liked to sit in that easy chair, and you can see the asbestos louvres in the window behind her quite clearly. Those louvres caused her death. She died of peritoneal mesothelioma. Let me tell you, it's the most awful disease.'

Summer is approaching, and with it comes the promise of months of sunshine and blue skies. Among the men and women waiting for medical appointments today, there are some who sense that this summer will be their last. They gaze vacantly at the passing traffic, their thoughts far away. They are thinking of the summers they will not see and the families they must leave behind.

In Australia, the James Hardie saga has continued to cause uncertainty for asbestos victims. Hardie made its voluntary compensation agreement conditional upon receiving tax concessions, but subsequently failed in its efforts to have the fund qualify as a charity. The company's fight to avoid paying business taxes on the fund threatened to undo the compensation deal and delayed its finalisation by two years.

The Hardie executives regarded as responsible for contriving to underfund the original compensation fund, the Medical Research and Compensation Foundation, received substantial payouts when they left the company. Mr Peter Macdonald, for example, the company's chief executive officer at the time, was given a $9 million payout and a $13,000 per month consultancy fee. Macdonald and other key players in the Hardie asbestos compensation debacle are living in virtual exile, their reputations severely diminished as a result of the findings of the special inquiry into the Medical Research and Compensation Foundation.

The story of James Hardie's treatment of its asbestos victims is not over yet.

Worldwide, the incidence of asbestos disease is on the rise, but in many developing countries where asbestos is produced and used, little is known of its dangers. As a consequence, there is a lack of data on the incidence of asbestos diseases. Without reliable statistics, we cannot determine the full extent of the international asbestos disaster.

Mesothelioma data are available for only 15 per cent of the world's population. Meagre though they are, these figures indicate that disease rates are highest in areas where asbestos use has been high, and that the people most at risk were employed in asbestos industries, shipyards and ports. The data also show that intensity of exposure is a factor – the greater the dust density, the higher the risk of contracting mesothelioma.

In countries where national mesothelioma registries exist, such as Australia, Britain and Italy, asbestos industries have disappeared, but in parts of the world where asbestos is mined, for example, in Russia, China, India, Kazakhstan, Zimbabwe and Brazil, data on the incidence of mesothelioma are virtually non-existent. There is also a dearth of information in countries where asbestos consumption is spiralling upwards, such as Indonesia, Thailand and Vietnam.

What little information we do have about mesothelioma indicates that the disease is on the rise all over the world.

In Japan, where asbestos consumption peaked in the 1970s, there has recently been a marked increase in the incidence of mesothelioma. Epidemiologists predict that the disease will have killed as many as 103,000 Japanese between 2000 and 2039.

South Korea will experience a similar catastrophe. The use of asbestos rose sharply in Korea during the 1970s to supply the industries driving the country's rapid economic growth – construction, shipbuilding and the manufacture of automobiles.

Indonesia, Thailand and Vietnam are experiencing a surge in construction activity, creating strong demand for the cheap, asbestos-based roof tiles produced locally. Thousands of people have been exposed to deadly dust at tile manufacturing plants and on construction sites, so large numbers of asbestos casualties are inevitable.

The Indian asbestos industry has the backing of the government. It operates about forty mines and hundreds of manufacturing plants employing more than 100,000 people. Most of these workers are illiterate and may face starvation if they do not have a job. In India, the asbestos industry is thriving.

Pakistan's asbestos industry is also robust, and the workers at its hundreds of mining, milling and manufacturing operations are largely illiterate too. The government of Pakistan does not recognise asbestos diseases, nor does it regulate occupational exposure to asbestos dust.

In Bangladesh, ship-breaking is a growth industry employing 80,000 workers, most of them illiterate. There is no monitoring of occupational health at the country's shipyards, about thirty altogether, and no restrictions on the handling of asbestos materials.

In Latin America, corporations based in the United States and Europe dominate the asbestos industries of Mexico, Brazil, Venezuela, Colombia and Peru. The South American workers employed in these industries come from poor backgrounds and tend to be compliant, because they are grateful to have a job. Brazil is different. Asbestos victims there have been tenacious in fighting European multinationals for compensation.

The South African asbestos mining and manufacturing industries that began at the beginning of the twentieth century benefited greatly from the apartheid regime. The efforts of black workers, including women and children, allowed these industries to prosper, and rich dividends were paid to company shareholders, many of them British. In the early 1960s, reports emerged of a high incidence of mesothelioma among black South African workers, particularly among those who had been employed at blue asbestos mines and in the shipbuilding and construction industries.

The asbestos industry has been important in Canada since the late 1800s. The Canadian government supports the industry, making it all the more difficult for people injured by asbestos to obtain compensation. About 80 per cent of Canadian asbestos mines are in the French-speaking province of Quebec, where unemployment is relatively high, and mine workers have no real employment alternatives. The weak position of its workforce strengthens the hand of the Canadian asbestos industry when workers seek to improve their conditions.

In Britain, more than 2500 people are dying of asbestos

disease each year, and mesothelioma mortality continues to increase. It is estimated that asbestos exposure will have killed 250,000 Britons between 1995 and 2029.

The incidence of asbestos disease in the United Kingdom is highest in areas where shipbuilding and other heavy industries once flourished – in East London, Liverpool, Cardiff, Glasgow and the Clydebank, Belfast, Tyneside, the smaller Scottish port cities of Leith and Aberdeen, and in York, where asbestos was used to insulate the railway carriages built there.

Large quantities of asbestos fire retardant materials were used in London's underground rail network. Problems associated with the presence of asbestos in rail tunnels came to light following the July 2005 terrorist bombings in London's public transport system. The forensic experts who investigated the aftermath of a bomb explosion on a train travelling underground encountered a danger they had not anticipated. In addition to contending with the stench, 60 degree heat, rotting corpses and proliferation of rats, the investigation teams working below Kings Cross railway station found that they risked inhaling carcinogenic dust. They reported that the fire proofing material in the tunnel had been damaged in the explosion and that the air around them was full of asbestos dust.

Asbestos has also been widely used on the continent of Europe. It was mined in Cyprus, Greece, France, Italy and Poland, and significant manufacturing industries existed in Italy and in northern France where the British conglomerate Turner & Newall ran a number of operations.

Construction industries all over Europe made extensive use of asbestos cement in the post-war period. Significant quantities of asbestos are contained in buildings erected decades ago and in underground transit networks such as the Metro in Paris. From the mature economies of Scandinavia to the heavily industrialised nations of northern

Europe, and from the emerging economies of Eastern Europe to the Catholic countries on the Iberian Peninsula and around the Mediterranean, asbestos is exacting a heavy toll. Europeans are dying as a result of the long period of asbestos activity, but Europe has a poor record of compensating victims. Even in Italy and France, where asbestos industries existed for most of the twentieth century, victims have rarely sued successfully for compensation.

In the United States, tens of thousands of people have been employed by asbestos companies, but the American asbestos industry is determined to protect itself against compensation claims. Industry strategies for avoiding liability include filing for bankruptcy and underfunding the trust funds set up to compensate victims. These strategies have proved effective. Claimants in the United States must fight hard for compensation and may receive only a few hundred dollars if successful.

The International Labour Organisation estimates that 100,000 people die in the world each year because they worked with asbestos, but the figure would be much higher if it included those who inhaled asbestos dust in or near their homes. This estimate by the International Labour Organisation suggests that the global asbestos death toll so far is in the hundreds of thousands and will eventually reach the millions. Bans and restrictions on the use of asbestos in the First World will not halt the rise of asbestos disease in developing countries. This is an international disaster which only a worldwide strategy can contain.

The horrors of asbestos disease have alarmed people around the world, and the calls for change are being heard. The injustice that asbestos victims have suffered has spurred some to come together in organised groups to campaign for their rights, but the enemy they face is formidable and often elusive, hidden behind complex corporate structures straddling different countries, where legislative regimes governing occupational health and safety can differ widely.

The international asbestos industry is mustering allies from within governments, the insurance industry and the legal and medical professions. It is drawing upon the support of the rich and powerful, including the President of the United States, who has made clear his intention to take asbestos litigation out of the courts. It is an industry well armed and systematically aggressive in defending legal actions taken against it, as companies such as James Hardie and CSR in Australia and the Manville Corporation in the United States have demonstrated.

Opposing forces are gathering to do battle on every continent, in countries rich and poor. The asbestos industry is fighting to avoid paying out billions of dollars to compensate people it has harmed and restore environments it has polluted. Its adversaries are ordinary working people prepared to take on the mighty forces in industry and government that have exploited and deceived them then cast them aside. The anti-asbestos forces are battling to compel the asbestos industry to meet its legal and moral obligations, to bring an end to all asbestos enterprises and to redress the chronic underfunding of medical research into asbestos disease. They will need the support of the societies in which they live if they are to achieve these goals.

In the end, individual societies will decide whether or not it is acceptable to let people die of asbestos diseases. The choice is theirs, and the question they will have to answer is this: Are they willing to risk lives unnecessarily by exposing people to asbestos in homes, schools, workplaces, or anywhere at all?

EPILOGUE

The implementation of the $1.5 billion asbestos compensation deal that James Hardie agreed to in December 2004 proved protracted. The stalling and wrangling continued, but in the final agreement the company tripled its original offer.

In February 2007, James Hardie shareholders voted at an extraordinary meeting held in Amsterdam in the Netherlands in favour of the $4.5 billion asbestos compensation fund allowing for payouts over forty years.

Bernie Banton, the man who spearheaded the public campaign to secure adequate compensation for asbestos victims from James Hardie, was among the first to receive a payout from the fund. A six-year stint at a Hardie factory in Sydney in the sixties and seventies caused Banton to suffer from asbestosis for many years, and he died of peritoneal mesothelioma in November 2007. His was a tenacious and inspiring campaign, fought for others when he himself was very ill. Banton was determined to ensure that Hardie's asbestos victims would be recompensed for the hardships they endured, and he succeeded.

The James Hardie fund marks a landmark compensation deal, providing relief and restitution to some asbestos victims in Australia and offering hope to people around the world whose lives have been shattered by asbestos.

Wakefield Press is an independent publishing and
distribution company based in Adelaide, South Australia.
We love good stories and publish beautiful books.
To see our full range of titles, please visit our website at
www.wakefieldpress.com.au.